RISE

PRAISE FOR *RISE*

"Trip's written a book that I think every young person needs to read. His passion for Jesus and this generation comes through loud and clear on every page. I can't wait to see the impact this message has on a generation that's hungry for purpose."

— Lecrae, Grammy awarding-
winning artist @lecrae

"*Rise* is a phenomenal book that captures the heart of our culture. As soon as I picked it up I couldn't put it down. Trip challenges you to be REAL, and shows you how to live your life as a young adult in the world today. Great read."

— Sam Acho, NFL linebacker,
humanitarian @thesamacho

"Trip has written a book I wish I would've read when I was younger. His passion, wisdom, and desire to challenge the younger generation is a testament to the work God's doing through Trip and the work he can do through us all."

— Kirk Franklin, Grammy award-
winning and multi-platinum
recording artist @kirkfranklin

"I loved reading *Rise*. Many times in this book I found myself meditating over pages after I read them. I was encouraged, inspired, and challenged all the way through. The culture expects us to waste time but God wants us to use our time for impact no matter our age. This is an amazing read for those who want to use their time wisely and make a difference for the Kingdom."

— Justin Forsett, NFL running
back @JForsett

"So often we talk about wanting to make a difference, but we don't actually get up and do anything. My buddy, Trip Lee, has written a book that will light a fire under a generation that's taught to take the easy way out. He's challenged us to 'rise' and live in the story that God's created for us. I know I'll be recommending this book to everyone I know."

— Stephen Curry, NBA player
@stephencurry30

RISE

Get Up and Live in God's Great Story

TRIP LEE

NELSON
BOOKS

An Imprint of Thomas Nelson

Published in Nashville, Tennessee, by Nelson Books, an imprint of Thomas Nelson. Nelson Books and Thomas Nelson are registered trademarks of HarperCollins Christian Publishing, Inc.

Thomas Nelson titles may be purchased in bulk for educational, business, fund-raising, or sales promotional use. For information, please e-mail SpecialMarkets@ThomasNelson.com.

Unless otherwise noted, Scripture quotations are taken from THE ENGLISH STANDARD VERSION. © 2001 by Crossway Bibles, a division of Good News Publishers.

Scripture quotations marked NIV are from the Holy Bible, New International Version®, NIV®. Copyright © 1973, 1978, 1984, 2011 by Biblica, Inc.™ Used by permission of Zondervan. All rights reserved worldwide. www.zondervan.com

Library of Congress Cataloging-in-Publication Data

Trip Lee, 1987–
  Rise : get up and live in God's great story / Trip Lee.
    pages cm
  Includes bibliographical references.
  ISBN 978-0-529-12099-1
  1. Trip Lee, 1987– 2. Christian biography. 3. Christian life. I. Title.
  BR1725.T675A3 2015
  277.3'083092—dc23
  [B]   2014023687

Printed in the United States of America

15 16 17 18 19 RRD 6 5 4 3 2 1

To Q and Selah

I'm praying God will raise you up for His glory at a young age.

CONTENTS

CONTENTS

FOREWORD

John Piper

One of the main things I like about Trip Lee and his book, *Rise*, is the interplay of reverence and relevance.

The aim at relevance in American culture is common. Cool is ubiquitous. As Mack Stiles says, Most Christians in the world must fear the raised fist; Americans fear the raised eyebrow. It means we are not cool. Not relevant.

But the aim at reverence is rare. Reverence feels old. It

feels unexciting. It's not cool. But everybody knows, deep down, that when reverence goes, all of human life becomes a variety show. Thin. Glib. Shallow. Plastic. Empty. In the end, meaningless.

We were made for more. "Cool is fickle, and we can't live for it"—the words of Trip Lee. Exactly. Trying to live just to be cool, just to be relevant, is low. And Trip Lee's voice cries out, *Rise!*

There is so much more to see, to know, to love, to enjoy. There are realities that are so great they can't be reduced to fun. The words "fun" "blast" "ball" "party" sound silly in the presence of the greatest and most awesome realities. Our vocabulary of joy has been reduced to "fun" because our taste buds for true majesty have died.

Trip says, "When it comes to morality, all of us have bad taste." Yes. And when it comes to God we have no taste. As Trip says, "It's common for eyes to light up when we talk about pop culture, but glaze over when we talk about Christ." The hills of culture are fun. The Himalayas of Christ are faint.

Trip Lee wants you to know: There is more than hills. Even for young adults there is more. This book is written for those who are young. It is written to give hope to those who feel they have little to contribute. It is written with the conviction that when a young person sees the glory of God everything changes. They *Rise!*

But the book is mature. It values the mature. It respects age. Trip is wise beyond his years. He sees already what years teach. Every breath is a gift. Every moment a trust.

"Wasting time is insanity. It's like burning money. The only difference is you can make more money, but you can never make more time."

I call this a reverence for what counts. Life is precious. And short. Trip is calling you to live for what counts. To live passionately, joyfully. Beyond silly. Beyond cool and clever.

If we are to rise on the Himalayan paths into the glory of God, we must know the way and not slip. "Shallow roots lead to shaky footing, so if we want to stand firm we have to go deep." Trip is leading you there. Go deep with him in order to go high. *Rise.*

INTRODUCTION

Letter to the Reader

Dear reader,

Thanks for picking up this book. I appreciate you taking some time to hear what I have to say. Before you start, let me tell you a little bit about myself. I grew up in Dallas, Texas, where God saved me from my sins as a teenager. As my life changed and I began to grow, He gave me a deep passion to share His truth with others. Since then I've been trying to share it in as many ways as I can.

One of the major ways I've done that is through my music. Music was my first love, and I've had the chance to put out several albums over the years. My desire to tell others about God is what led me to write. I'm also one of the pastors at my church, where I help teach, counsel, and coordinate ministry to the youth. I'm the founder of BRAG, a ministry dedicated to connecting a diverse young crowd with biblically solid content, and I blog regularly at BuiltToBrag.com. As I write this book, I'm in my midtwenties, I've been married for five years, and I have two young kids.

I want you to know who I am because I write from a very personal perspective. I've tried to write each chapter in a conversational way so the book would be easy and natural to read. I want to focus on God's Word and point you to it, but I don't want the book to feel like a really long sermon—which is definitely hard because I'm 95 percent preacher and 5 percent everything else.

This book is mainly aimed at young Christians. If you're not a Christian, I'm still glad you picked it up. I want this book to be one that skeptics and seekers can enjoy and understand as well. And you can define "young" however you wish.

I'm not writing this book because I think I've figured it all out. I'm still on the journey, too, so I want it to feel like a discussion with a fellow seeker who's trying to play his part in God's story. The book doesn't hit everything we need to know by any means, but I've written about the things God has put on my heart.

I believe God has taught me many things from His Word,

and I want to share some of them with you. But I want you to think of me as sitting across the table from you having coffee instead of standing at the front of a classroom lecturing. I pray that when we're finished with our coffee, you'll be encouraged to rise. I try not to take myself too seriously, so you'll notice I crack a few jokes here and there. If you don't think I'm that funny, that's okay, because my wife does. Moving on.

I want you to know what to expect as you trek through these pages. The book is split into three main sections: getting up, growing up, and pointing up. The first section talks about what it means for each of us to embrace our role in God's story and rise to the calling. The second section talks about how to grow in the roles God has shown us. And the final section talks about how our rising points people to the glory of the God who raises people from the dead. I try to approach each of these areas with consideration of the unique struggles of young people like you and me.

If I had to sum up this book in one sentence, it would be this: *get up and live*. That's my sincere prayer for you. I hope this book encourages you in that direction.

Trip Lee

• Part One •

GETTING UP

1

7:00 A.M. LOGIC

I was fifteen years old and my life was being turned inside out. My name and appearance hadn't changed, but everything else about me had. I was a completely different person than I had been a year or two before. I don't mean like when people go to college and re-create themselves with new nicknames and personalities; I mean something significant had gone on inside of me. I had become a Christian. I felt new. I felt alive.

I felt so good that I had to announce it to anyone who

would listen, especially my closest friends and family. Everyone responded differently to the change in me—some with joy, others with resistance—but one conversation has always stood out to me.

I was talking with an older man whom I greatly respected, thrilled to explain my game plan for honoring God with my lifestyle, specifically my sexual purity. I tried to be calm about it, but it was always hard to hold my excitement in. As the words leapt from my tongue at an unnatural pace, I got the sense that he wasn't as excited as I was. He was trying to listen quietly, but his facial expression responded before his mouth had a chance. He seemed halfway amused and halfway concerned.

He gave me a confused look and calmly asked, "Why are you taking life so seriously, young man? Why are you trying so hard to do everything right? Youth is the time when you mess up a lot, and that's okay. Just enjoy yourself, learn from those mistakes, and get serious when you get older."

I was stunned. Some might have taken that advice as liberating and honest, but that's not how it felt to me. It felt constraining and misleading. I knew what he said was wrong, but I was a new Christian and I couldn't quite put it into words.

I reflected on that experience for a long time, but instead of dampening my fire, I think it turned up the heat. I didn't know much at the time, but I knew I couldn't just sit around and wait. I had to get up and live.

OUR FAULTY LOGIC

Waking up is my least favorite part of every day. It's not that I don't appreciate a new day with new opportunities, but getting out of bed just never seems appealing. Ever. When it's eleven at night, getting in bed is just an ordinary part of my day. But when it's seven in the morning, staying in bed is like winning the lottery.

If you look at my iPhone, you'll see that, sadly, I have about sixteen alarms set in fifteen-minute increments starting just before 7:00 a.m. Why? Because there's pretty much no chance I'll get up after the thirteenth alarm. Those next three—numbers fourteen, fifteen, and sixteen—are my only chance to actually have a day.

Sometimes I think I could convince myself of anything in those first drowsy minutes of each morning. This was at its worst during my college years, when climbing out of bed in the morning felt like climbing Mount Everest without any legs. I could tell myself all kinds of lies, like, "Yeah, you should go to class, but will it really matter?" or "I know you've been late every day for the last three weeks, but what's another day?" or "Maybe my friend will take the test for me. It's worth the risk." Sad, I know. That's what I call 7:00 a.m. logic.

The lie I told myself was that staying in bed would be good for me. Somehow an extra five minutes or an extra hour would improve my life. When I'm wide awake it seems foolish, but in those first moments of each day it seems perfectly logical.

Can you imagine what the world would be like if nobody got up until they felt like it? Businesses would fold, schools would suffer, the government would be even more chaotic than it already is. Nobody would have enough time to do his job well; by the time everyone woke up, half the day would be gone. The truth is, no matter what time you decide to rise from your slumber, you only have twenty-four hours to work with. Hitting the snooze button doesn't actually buy you any extra time. Your work just won't get done.

Unfortunately, many of us have adopted 7:00 a.m. logic as a way of life. We sometimes call it procrastination. We don't feel like doing something in the moment, so we decide to put it off until later. Sometimes we do it with small things, like taking out the trash, studying for a test, answering work e-mails, or returning Mom's phone call.

But procrastination doesn't actually solve anything, so it's a bad idea to delay daily tasks until the last minute. It's an even worse idea to delay life itself.

WHAT DO YOU EXPECT?

Let's be honest. Our culture doesn't usually expect much from people until they're old. (I'll avoid offending anybody and let you define *old*.) According to many, youth isn't the time for great responsibility or expectation. They say, "You'll bear the burdens of responsibility for the rest of your life, so enjoy your youth while you can!" People seem to expect us to take all of life lightly until we reach that magical, arbitrary age of responsibility. Is it eighteen? Is it twenty-one? Is it thirty? Your guess is as good as mine.

I had a conversation with a waiter in Phoenix one night not too long ago. He wasn't much younger than me, probably in his early twenties. He was really friendly from the moment I sat down, and we ended up having a good conversation. I asked him all the usual small-talk questions: Where are you from? How long have you worked here? Will you spit in my food?

As he responded to my questions, it was clear that he'd bought into the 7:00 a.m. logic. He told me that he had only lived in Phoenix for a few months. Before that he was in Nevada, before that California, and before that he lived on the East Coast. At this point I began asking myself how I'd describe him to a police sketch artist, just in case he was a fugitive of some sort.

But when I asked him why he moved around so much, here's what he told me: "Just because. I don't want to stay in one place and take on a bunch of responsibility. I'm young, man. It's my time to just explore, not be bogged down with a bunch of commitments. Who knows, maybe I'll find myself."

I was sad but not surprised by his response. Of course there's nothing wrong with moving a lot or self-discovery, but is there a season in our early twenties—or even our teens—when life doesn't really matter? Should we hold off on all convictions, commitments, and seriousness until later?

CAN YOU TRUST IT?

I heard a song the other day that captured this perspective perfectly. The lyric went, "We're happy, free, confused, and lonely at the same time."[1]

I know taking on Taylor Swift hasn't gone well for people in the past (do I need to remind you about Kanye?). But I'm willing to take the risk and examine what she says in her song "22." I know it's just a fun song, so I don't want to over-analyze it. I think she has successfully captured the feelings of her listeners and the spirit of the age. But the perspective is all wrong.

What does it mean, as she says in the song, to "feel twenty-two"? The song celebrates the kind of carefree, light, and easy young adulthood that many of us dreamed about. Unfortunately, it suggests that this happiness and freedom is found in confused, sometimes miserable wander-ings. There's no direction, no responsibility—just chaotic fun. It's that 7:00 a.m. logic again. Who has time for life when you feel twenty-two? Swift didn't make this perspec-tive up; we've been sold this logic over and over again. But can it be trusted?

Whether or not this 7:00 a.m. logic is trustworthy depends on who you are and what you were created for. If you were only created for self-satisfaction and enjoyment, then putting off real life until later may be the best choice. If you're noth-ing more than another person looking out for yourself, then that young waiter's logic may seem pretty sound. You can wait until later to wake up if you want to. But what if you were created for something more?

WHO ARE YOU?

All of us are born with a beautiful, naive joy. As babies, the world seems like a good place. Our needs are usually met, and each day brings new discoveries. I see this so clearly in my two-year-old son. It seems like he's happy for no reason. Eye contact makes him grin, and sudden movements provoke explosive laughter. As far as he knows, *all* of life is beautiful. Yes, he's traumatized at the thought of waiting five seconds for food, and he's already had a few scares in the hospital, but it hasn't fazed him. He seems to have a momentary memory that can go from intense tears to intense joy in seconds. But it won't always be so.

Reality hits all of us eventually. Naive joy and perceived innocence can only survive for so long in our world. It happens for some of us earlier than others, but all of us snap out of it and realize the truth—our world is a mess. Life is full of hardship. Something's not right.

We watch the news and feel that pit in our stomachs when we hear of tsunamis killing hundreds or thousands in other countries. We shudder when we hear deafening gunshots echo in our neighborhoods. We grieve when aggressive cancer invades the bodies of our relatives. We instinctively know that this is not how life was meant to be. And when we come to that discovery—whether at age two or twenty-two—we respond in different ways. We're forced to ask ourselves where we fit in all of this mess.

Some of us think too highly of ourselves. In our pride we think this wrongness, this evil chaos, is only outside of us. We assume that we've escaped the destruction, as if we were in a house on fire and didn't get burned.

Others of us think too lowly of ourselves. We know we're not perfect. As a matter of fact, we think everyone around us is aware of our shortcomings too. Our lives don't matter that much, so it's pointless to think deeply about how we should live. Maybe God cares about us, but if so, it's hard to tell.

Both these perspectives miss the mark, and both can lead to delaying true life instead of embracing it.

The truth is, we're not perfect and we're not worthless. The Bible tells us that we're beautifully made, but broken. Our flawless Creator made us in His image (Gen. 1:27). He thought us up, carefully crafted our frames, and breathed life into us. And after God created the world, including mankind, He took a step back, admired His handiwork, and called it "very good" (Gen. 1:31).

But it didn't stay that way. Sin entered the world, and since then everything has been a mess. Our world is sick, and none of us are immune to the infection. At our cores we're sinners. We purposely rebel against our Creator. We were made to be mirrors perfectly reflecting God's goodness, but with sin that mirror was fractured and the reflection is distorted.

Instead of following God, we assume we're wiser and follow our own misguided intuition. We're choosing what we think will make us happy, but in the process we've made God angry. He despises sin and He will judge us for it. We're beautifully made, but tragically broken.

The good news is that we can be put back together. God sent Jesus to repair our relationship with Him and to restore His image in us. The only way we could escape God's judgment was if Jesus took it for us. We owe more than we can pay. On the cross, He paid the death debt for sinners, and He rose three days later to give us new life. If we let go of our sin and trust in Him, our old self can die with Him and a brand-new version of us can rise.

If you haven't rejected your sin and embraced the Savior, I plead with you to do so. The only way you can rise is if you rise with Him. Otherwise, we're doomed to a dead life that really can't be called life at all. If you're not convinced yet, that's okay. I'd love for you to keep reading and consider what it would look like to get up and live for the first time.

If you've submitted yourself to Jesus, your new life has already begun. There's no in-between phase where we just exist in a youth, college, or young singles ministry. You're a real human being, a real follower of Christ, a real world-changer right now. If you've been given new life, why would you wait to start walking in it? It's a new day, the sun is shining in the window, and we should rise early instead of sleeping in.

BEFORE IT GETS UGLY

Sometimes saying it gently doesn't work and we need a dose of realness to wake us up. It doesn't get any more real than Ecclesiastes. In this short book, the author (probably Solomon) talked about the realities of life in our messed-up world. He had lived it all, seen it all, and done it all. Reading Ecclesiastes is kind of like talking to a wise but grumpy old man sitting in a rocking chair on the porch, telling you everything he's learned. He wants you to live a full life and not make the same mistakes he did.

The experienced preacher closed out his appeal with some blunt counsel for how to view our youth: "Remember also your Creator in the days of your youth, before the evil days come and the years draw near of which you will say, 'I have no pleasure in them'" (Eccl. 12:1).

He didn't say we should ignore God for now and get serious later. He said the opposite. He urged us to fear God and live for Him while we're still young. And he said we should do it "before the evil days come." I think he meant before we get old and life gets harder. A day will come when our lives won't be nearly as carefree, so we should give it all we have right now.

After verse 1, the preacher in Ecclesiastes begins to tell us what those evil days will look like. Honestly, it's kind of depressing. It seems like he is poetically describing the breakdown of our bodies. Reading it is like watching a plane plummet from the sky, knowing that it will inevitably crash into the ground.

One day our bodies will start to shut down. Our eyes won't work the same and our minds won't be as sharp. If we make it to old age, most of us will be a lot more limited in our capabilities. What good does it do to put off all the hard work until we can't actually do it? And what makes us think we'll actually want to do it then? The myth of procrastination is that it will somehow be easier later. The truth is, it's never easy, and putting it off only makes it harder.

There are great benefits to living for Jesus in the present. Now is the time when we have the most strength. Now is the time when we have the most energy. Now is the time when we can give it everything we have. Now is the time to get up and live.

THANKS, BUT NO THANKS

Over the years I've reflected on the conversation I told you about at the beginning of the chapter. At the time I didn't know how to put my objection into words. How do you think I should have responded? If somehow I got the chance to go back to that moment, here's what I would say to my friend:

"Thank you so much for speaking into my life and trying to help me find my way. I know you're older, more responsible, and more mature than me in many ways. I respect you more than I can say, but I strongly disagree with your counsel. I know you meant well, but I'm actually a little offended by it.

"Your assertion that I shouldn't take my life seriously yet was unintentionally belittling. It assumes that nothing is required of me now. It assumes that my life and decision making aren't that important at the moment. Basically, it assumes that I'm not a real person quite yet.

"I reject that. I'll never be perfect, but I will not embrace my sins as mere growing pains. God created me to show Him off, and He's called me to give my life to Him. I know I could try to wait until later, but I intend to do it now. I have the choice between sleeping in or getting up. I choose to rise."

2

THE LEBRON JAMES EFFECT

I had a monthly subscription to *ESPN The Magazine* when I was younger. Basketball had grown to be my favorite sport, so I was always excited when the cover story was something hoops related. One month I retrieved the oversized issue from the mailbox and turned it over to see a fresh young face on the cover. The player was reaching out to the camera with a cocky "I just dunked on you" look on his face.

The text under his chin read, "The Chosen One: High school junior LeBron James would be an NBA lottery pick right now." I scanned the caption and rolled my eyes. I had bought into the hype of a "chosen one" bypassing college for the pros before, but it was usually a letdown. Some young players, like Kobe Bryant, had successfully gone from high school graduate to NBA star, but even his greatness took a couple of seasons to blossom. I brushed it off, assuming I'd never think about LeBron again. The hype didn't die down, though.

The Cleveland Cavaliers selected LeBron James first in the draft, and as his first game approached, I didn't plan to pay it much attention. Instead of coming off the bench and making little impact on the game (as I expected), however, he was the starting small forward and his skills were on full display. He was dunking with style, hitting jump shots, and looking like a great player already. You could tell he was something special.

That year, at the age of nineteen, he gave hope to a struggling team, and within a few years he would lead them to the NBA finals. He rose to the occasion and lived up to the hype.

I would have been impressed with that kind of play from a longtime player, or maybe even a rookie who'd had his college years to mature, but I didn't expect it from a nineteen-year-old kid who had been taking calculus just a year before. He couldn't drink yet, but he could dunk on your favorite player. That made his achievements even more impressive, and he was the most exciting part of the NBA season that year.

Stories like this show that we look at accomplishments

not just because of the achievement itself, but also because of who's doing the achieving. The more unlikely the achiever, the more impressive it is.

We see this all the time in different spheres of life—music, sports, and many more. If a little kid can play three notes on the piano, people go crazy. We fawn over child prodigies and watch them on TV shows. Celebrities like Michael Jackson and Justin Bieber drew attention quickly, in part because of how young they were when they were discovered.

We're blown away when mature characteristics show up in immature packages. One of my favorite things about young talents is that they refuse to wait. They are gifted, and they intend to use that gifting right away. They want to be a part of the story now. There's a lesson to learn here. When young people accomplish great things, the accomplishment is even more impressive. It's the LeBron James effect.

LEARN YOUR LINES

Young people will be written off. Like the uncoordinated kid in gym class, we're the last ones people choose. We'll be written off and dismissed just like I wrote off LeBron James. I don't mean that people want us to fail; they just don't expect much from us. It's assumed that someone who hasn't had as much time to mature can't possibly play a significant role in the world yet. The bar for us is low, but that doesn't mean we have to accept it. We should rise above it.

In the first chapter, I argued that we are all wonderfully

made by God. But for what? God is first and foremost about His own fame, reputation, and glory in the world. A football player runs, blocks, catches, and tackles; but at the end of the day, he does it for the win. There's something great about a touchdown or a great tackle, but it means nothing without the win. It's the same with God. He creates and loves and saves, but ultimately it's for His glory. That's the end goal for God.

The psalms are a great illustration of this as they call on God's people to praise Him.

> *Praise the* LORD *from the earth,*
>   *you great sea creatures and all ocean depths,*
> *lightning and hail, snow and clouds,*
>   *stormy winds that do his bidding,*
> *you mountains and all hills,*
>   *fruit trees and all cedars,*
> *wild animals and all cattle,*
>   *small creatures and flying birds,*
> *kings of the earth and all nations,*
>   *you princes and all rulers on earth,*
> *young men and women,*
>   *old men and children.*
>   (Ps. 148:7–12 NIV)

Everything in creation exists for the same main purpose: praising the Lord. From sea creatures to bad weather, to wild animals, to rulers, even on down to young people like us.

God is a masterful Author telling the greatest story of all

time. He'll never win the Pulitzer Prize, but the story He's writing will be celebrated for all eternity. The story isn't just about man, or sin, or salvation; it's about Him. And all of us get to be a part of this grand story. The day you were born, you were written into the plot.

Whether you're young, old, rich, poor, healthy, or handicapped, you have a role to play. Yes, even you. Why waste the first chapters of your life on the wrong story? Join all creation in telling the greatest story of all time, under the authority of the Author of all things.

THE WEAKER, THE BETTER

There are several problems with writing off young people. One of them is the strange assumption that for some reason God can't get glory from young people. Are we so useless that even God can't figure out what to do with us? Nothing could be further from the truth. God loves to use the unexpected to do great things.

Have you seen those cooking shows where the hosts surprise the contestants with strange ingredients and ask them to make world-class meals? The hosts will say something like, "I want you to make a juicy steak and ice cream for dessert, using only oxygen and cardboard." And when the contestants do it, they show that they're incredibly skilled! It's the same with God using us. He loves using lackluster ingredients, because doing so makes it clear where the true credit should go.

In the Old Testament, God did this all the time with His

people Israel. It would be painfully clear that their army was no match for their enemies, but somehow they'd win. God went before them to make clear that He was the mighty one and not them. He deliberately left them weak to show that He was their strength. We, too, are young and weak in many ways, but that means we have an opportunity to show the world the source of true strength.

GODLINESS IS THE BEST RESPONSE

What do we do about those people who think we're worthless? Be an example for them. Paul gave instructions to his young colaborer about how to glorify God in his church: "Don't let anyone look down on you because you are young, but set an example for the believers in speech, in conduct, in love, in faith and in purity" (1 Tim. 4:12 NIV). Paul was saying that when people look down on you for being young, you should respond. He didn't say accept their assessment and wait until later to take action. He said don't let them get away with it.

Paul wasn't encouraging us to threaten older people or to go on Facebook rants; he was telling us to live godly lives. He told us to do so as an example for all believers, including those who look down on us. We should be mature and show others what it looks like to follow Christ, not in an arrogant way, but in a way that humbly shows the power of God at work.

So when people look down on you, be an example of grace to them. Pursue God. Love hard. Be pure. They'll be blown away that God would use a young person to show them what it looks like to follow Him. And God will get the glory.

JESUS AT TWELVE

I love seeing this dynamic in the life of our Lord. At just twelve years old, He already understood the things of God, and He began trying to grow. The young God-man was in the temple with the teachers. Luke said, "They found him in the temple courts, sitting among the teachers, listening to them and asking them questions. Everyone who heard him was amazed at his understanding and his answers" (2:46–47 NIV).

It seems the teachers weren't amazed just because they heard good answers, but also because of whom they heard the answers from. I'm pretty sure that when I was twelve I still wore shoes that lit up when I ran hard enough. But Jesus understood the role He was to play in God's story. He wasn't just another person like us; He was the God-man who came to save us. And He wasn't wasting any time.

RARE SIGHTINGS

The more rare something is, the more attention it draws. It's so rare that you meet somebody under the age of thirty who truly loves God and seeks Him with all they have. When I drive through different neighborhoods in DC, I see young people walking around and I wonder where they are at. Most are caught up in things that dishonor God, thus they rebel against their roles in the story.

I'm not shocked when I talk to a college student who cares nothing about God. It's not so surprising when I see someone on social media who claims to be a Christian but seems to be an example of recklessness instead of purity. It's common for eyes to light up when we talk about pop culture but glaze over when we talk about Christ. And it's grieving to me.

But God is at work. There are spiritual LeBrons all over the world, running toward God even though it's against the flow of traffic. They're being trained by the Word, they're getting stronger every day, and those around them are blown away.

It's powerful to see a young man in his early twenties who would rather spend time with God's people than go to a club. It's powerful to see a young man fighting to remain sober. It's powerful to see a young woman finding her identity in Christ and not in what others think. What an amazing picture of God's grace.

HE CAN DO IT

Maybe seeing young people living true life is so rare that you think it can't happen. You're aware of your weaknesses and all the reasons it'll be hard. But God does it all the time, and He can do it with you. His Spirit is powerful and mighty to save. God will use you because He delights to use unexpected things and people like you and me. And the "LeBron James effect" means the impact may be even greater than if it came from someone you expected it from.

Right now you have the opportunity to play a unique role in God's story. What are you waiting for? *Get up and live!*

3

DON'T ENVY THE BENCH

I played varsity basketball in high school. That's a completely true statement (unless you force me to define the word *play*). I attended a small private school, and if you were a senior you got a spot on the varsity team. I love the game of basketball, but I'm a lot better at watching it than playing it. I can chastise players and yell "C'mon!" at referees with all-star skill. But that's as far as it goes. My school had this strange rule about actually playing sports in order to graduate, though, so I was forced to suit up and hang my head in shame every Friday night.

The stands were always full for home games. Excited parents and students—many of them friends of mine—showed up to support the team. Sadly, they probably made as much of a difference in the game as I did. I would glance into the bleachers from time to time, wondering what all the people were thinking, especially my dad. I think he realized that both of us were just there to watch, but I happened to have a better seat.

The only time I actually made it onto the floor was at the very end of the game—you know, when they put in the guys they feel bad for. I like to tell myself they saved me for those final seconds so I could secure the win. As we shook hands with the opposing team after the final buzzer, I felt like the players were snickering inside when they looked at me and said, "Good game."

When I emerged from the locker room after my shower, nobody wanted a picture with me. None of the middle school kids looked up to me. Nobody on either team envied me. Why? Because I was more Spike Lee than Michael Jordan. I was a fan wearing a jersey. I was the guy who never made it into the game, and nobody envies the benchwarmer.

GET IN THE GAME

I can't ever remember somebody shooting a pretend air jumper and calling out the name of an unknown role player. Those guys are still professionals, but if you wish you could trade places with a basketball player, it's usually the starter, the guy who is out there from tip-off to final buzzer. You'll never forget when Jordan switched hands in midair or when Ray Allen hit that three at the buzzer. Those are the guys you want to be. They're in the action at those key moments, not just spectating. But for some reason we do the opposite when it comes to life. Everybody wants to be a benchwarmer.

What do I mean by that? If you showed up on a typical college campus and interviewed students about their goals for the semester, you wouldn't hear much about living for the King. You'd hear more about thoughtless fun than playing a role in the grand story. Maybe you'd even hear some 7:00 a.m. logic. I'm willing to assume you'd receive similar responses at a high school or an office building. All of us have goals and desires, but God isn't always in them.

I hope you don't take what I'm saying as judgmental condemnation. I'm not a movie critic trashing the acting; I'm a supporting actor trying to get my lines right too. I'd be lying if I said following Jesus always seems appealing. Right doesn't always feel right.

I remember a time, soon after I joined the staff at my church, when all my friends were going to perform at an incredible music festival. I wanted to be there so badly, but I couldn't make it because it fell during the first week of my new job. I had to fight the envy in my heart. Especially when I saw them posting pictures online of their amazing experiences.

Sometimes we feel that way with life. It's easy to envy others, especially when they're doing something great like my friends were doing. But even when we know people are living wrong, we sometimes find ourselves longing to join them. And that makes following Jesus feel like getting taken out of the game, not getting subbed in. But why do we envy others and assume we're missing out on something?

WHY DO WE THINK WE'RE MISSING OUT?

Bad Eyesight

One of our problems is that we can only see what's right in front of us. We miss the big picture. It's like a camera when the things in front are in focus and everything behind is blurry. We need to adjust our lenses so the entire picture will become clear.

There's not a person on this earth who doesn't struggle to see clearly. It's one of the consequences of our sinful hearts. But when you throw youthfulness into the equation, it adds up to disaster. One-year-olds struggle to walk well, and twenty-somethings struggle to see well.

It's not surprising. It's part of what it means to be young in a fallen world. Our lives have been brief and we've only seen so much. It's hard to imagine the whole puzzle when you've only seen three pieces. This doesn't mean we should flog ourselves in shame; but it does mean we should be aware, because sinful shortsightedness can lead to disaster.

Have you ever tried driving in a snowstorm? The Christmas after my first child was born, a terrible snowstorm hit as my wife and I drove back to DC from Pittsburgh. The snow overpowered the headlights on our SUV and fell so fast that the windshield wipers couldn't keep up with it. My knuckles turned white as I nervously gripped the wheel; I realized the lives of my wife and son were in my hands.

I was tense. I could only see a few inches in front of my face, so I literally didn't know where I was going. I didn't know what was ahead, and I just had to hope it would all work out. That's not a good feeling. I couldn't see if there was a car stopped ahead or a person wiping off his windows in the stop-and-go traffic.

I haven't even mentioned the slick roads yet. Hitting your brakes meant your car slid like a kid wearing socks on a tile floor. You can understand why it was my least favorite drive ever. I was shortsighted and in a slippery place.

Have you ever thought about how disastrous shortsightedness can be in our lives? If we only make decisions based on what's right in front of us, we're bound to run into danger. Too many of us are trying to live our lives with no regard for what happens later.

Getting drunk at a party may seem like a good idea in the moment, but it dishonors God and leads to stupid decisions. Sleeping with your boyfriend or girlfriend may seem like a win in the moment, but that kind of intimacy was never meant to be enjoyed apart from the unique union of a marriage.

We'll dive in to these types of decisions more as we go through the book, but the point is, we have to think big picture. Every decision we make is a small piece of a larger puzzle. And without looking at the big picture for reference, we'll place the pieces incorrectly every time. It's tragic to treasure a moment in time more than an entire lifetime.

Bad Taste

We all have that friend who dresses terribly, the one who looks over simple T-shirts while shopping and chooses to go for the tie-dyed, droopy-neck shirt with orange sequins. No sir. You don't have to be a fashion model, but you also don't have to wear your dad's jeans that were unacceptable even when he bought them twenty years ago.

Fashion sense is like a sixth sense some of us have and some of us don't. Some of us just have the instinct to put the right combinations together, even if they're simple. As you can probably tell, I assume I have it. And if you disagree with me about that, I'll pray for you.

When it comes to morality, all of us have bad taste. None of us is born with natural moral sense. None of us has that perfect combination of heart and deeds. Instead, we're repelled by good things and attracted to the wrong things. Because of this, when we don't get to take part in wickedness, we feel like we're being left out. We feel like we're missing out on the fun. But we have it exactly backward.

Strangely, we complain about missing the chance to waste our lives. That's like complaining about being spared in a deadly hostage situation. There are some times when it's better to be left out.

Sometimes it does seem like the entire world is going in one direction and God is asking us to go the other way. And it wouldn't be so hard to follow Him if everyone didn't seem like they were having such a good time.

Friends, Satan is a master at false advertising. He convinces us that pain feels good and salt tastes sweet. But those commercials he shows leave out the fine print, and those images we see are photoshopped. We don't have to believe the hype. Even when he offers us something persuasive, we should trust God's taste over our own.

Bad Theology

Last year I spoke at an event for college students and tried to answer this question: Does becoming a Christian mean I can't have fun? I thought it was an important question to ask because so many assume the answer is yes. While I was glad to address it, I was also struck by how confused we are. Christianity has an ugly reputation, and it shows how badly we've misunderstood God.

To rephrase the question, it's basically asking: Does God want you to have a boring life? To answer yes is to say something untrue about Him. He's the Creator of life, and it's tragic to suggest that He might not want you to enjoy it.

That's like wondering if Jay-Z wants you to like his newest album. Does he want you to just suffer through it and hate it? Or like asking if Steven Spielberg wanted you to doze off because you hated *Lincoln* so much. Well, of course not! They made the album and movie, in part, so that others would enjoy them.

Life is different, because it's not just some form of

entertainment, but there are similarities. God is a good God. He created life, and He wants us to live that life to the fullest.

There's nothing in the Bible that suggests God doesn't want you to enjoy anything. That's just not the picture you'll get when you read the Scriptures. The way people talk about Christianity, you'd think there was a verse where Jesus says, "If you follow Me, you must be miserable forever, hate everything, and drag others down with you." While He does call us to some difficult things, a miserable eternity is not one of them.

We often assume God wants to keep us from good things, but that's a lie. Think about what James, the brother of Jesus, said in his letter: "Do not be deceived, my beloved brothers. Every good gift and every perfect gift is from above, coming down from the Father of lights with whom there is no variation or shadow due to change" (James 1:16–17).

God doesn't try to keep us from good things; He's the giver of all good things. He's the source. Asking if He wants us to enjoy those good things is like an orphan wondering if the benefactors who provide her with food and shelter want her to have good things. How can you ask that question when they've provided all the good things you have? It's an illogical question. God created friendship and marriage. God created smiling and laughter. To act like He doesn't want us to enjoy them is ridiculous.

Recently, my wife and I went to see a movie about outer space in IMAX 3-D. When you arrive, they give you a pair of those clunky glasses to make sure you get the full effect. But what if, instead of wearing those glasses, we brought our sleep masks from home? Those are meant to block out all the light around you, so you can see nothing but darkness and sleep in peace.

If we were to put on our sleep masks, we'd miss the whole movie. But since we put on the 3-D glasses they provided, it was amazing. It was like we were in outer space with the characters. Stars were around us and debris was flying at us. The glasses brought that experience to life. I started holding my drink down, hoping it wouldn't float up into the air.

Sadly, we treat God like He's handing us sleep masks in the movies, when really He's handing us the 3-D goggles. He's not trying to block our joy and leave us in the dark. He intends to enhance our joy, to give us fullness of joy. He wants us to enjoy life as it was meant to be enjoyed.

As we'll talk about in a later chapter, becoming a Christian does mean you'll have to deny yourself some things that seem enjoyable in the moment. But when you understand God's plan for your joy, you'll know it's worth it. And soon you'll find those things don't seem so enjoyable after all.

THE SOLUTION

So far we've talked about the problem quite a bit: we feel like we're missing out, and it's because we have soul issues. But what do we do to fix them?

One of the things I love about the Bible is how realistic it is. That may sound crazy to some people, but it's true. It's impossible to read the Bible and walk away feeling like you're the only person with issues. There is no struggle we experience that we can't find a similar experience in the Scriptures.

In Psalm 73, we see a little bit of benchwarmer envy from Asaph. Asaph began the psalm reminding readers of God's goodness and contrasting that with himself. He said, "My feet had almost slipped; I had nearly lost my foothold" (v. 2 NIV).

Asaph wanted to stand as a man of God, but he almost slipped and fell. He was almost knocked off the right path. He almost completely lost sight. Why? He said in verse 3, "For I envied the arrogant when I saw the prosperity of the wicked" (NIV). Asaph saw what the wicked had, and he wanted it.

Asaph was talking about those who live their lives with disregard for God and live in a way that offends Him. And Asaph felt like they had all the fun and all the stuff. He became obsessed with what other people had. He couldn't understand why a God who was in control would allow the wicked to prosper while the righteous suffered.

But by the end of the psalm, his vision was corrected. What changed? We need to get hold of whatever Asaph got hold of that helped him to see clearly again.

He saw God. He was with God. He said he was in the sanctuary, and then his perspective shifted. When we focus on the wicked, it seems like they have everything. But when we look at our God, we see the truth. He's all we need.

This was Asaph's perspective after he was with God: "Whom have I in heaven but you? And earth has nothing

I desire besides you. My flesh and my heart may fail, but God is the strength of my heart and my portion forever" (Ps. 73:25–26 NIV).

IT'S GAME TIME

Sometimes I'll have conversations with friends who had very different pasts from me. They'll tell stories about how messed up they were and how dazed they were after trying new drugs. By God's grace, I've never been high, intoxicated, or imprisoned—which is a good thing. But sometimes I'm tempted to feel left out, like my life has been lame. When I really think about it, though, God was gracious to keep me from having those memories. The only thing I really missed out on was unnecessary heartbreak and wasted time.

Whenever I talk to older Christians, they'll often say, "I wish I had been following Christ when I was your age! I wasted a lot of time on nonsense." I've never talked to an older Christian who was grateful for the years they spent rebelling against God. When our lives come to an end, we won't be disappointed that we missed out on things that didn't matter.

I want to encourage you to rise. Get off the bench and get into the game. And if you're already in the game, keep pushing even when you get fatigued. There's a great reward after the final buzzer.

4

THERE ARE NO SUPER-CHRISTIANS

I became a Christian right as I was entering high school. For
the longest time I'd assumed I was a Christian, not only
because I went to church with my family, but also because I
liked Jesus. I considered myself a Christian in the same way
I considered myself black—my parents were, so I must be as
well. After all, we didn't follow Hinduism, atheism, or any
other belief system. But soon I would learn that even those

born in Christian homes have to be born again. Even church kids have to be converted.

When I was around fourteen years old, the Lord set me up to have my prior worldview obliterated. I had begun to attend the youth services at the mega Baptist church my family attended. I usually tell people I started going to youth group for social reasons—which is a nice way to say I wanted to get to know some of the girls. Despite my questionable motives, God used my time in that youth group to give me new life. The youth pastor had far better motives than I did, and he preached the good news about forgiveness available in Jesus.

The lightbulb came on and everything clicked in a new way. I finally saw my mess and trusted Jesus to clean it up. There was a lot of junk to deal with, but I knew Jesus could do anything. Immediately after my conversion I experienced some genuine life change, but it wasn't until my sophomore year in high school that my life was visibly different to others.

As I began to grow, so did my discomfort about some of the things I did. God showed me numerous ways I'd been dishonoring Him with my life. One of those ways was how I viewed girls. I was disturbed by the way I'd treated them in the past, and I wanted to do better. I started trying to respect them, to treat them as precious beings created in God's image and not as moving objects for me to gawk at. I had a long way to go, but I was headed in the right direction. Was I serious about changing the way I looked at women? A real test was coming.

I was in chemistry class one day, and I wanted to stab

myself in the eye because I was even worse at chemistry than I was at geometry. Good thing God wasn't sending me a chemistry test, because I surely would have failed. As I contemplated what tool I would use to harm myself, a friend tapped me on the shoulder and pointed. I thought he had read my mind and was showing me a pointy object, but he was actually pointing at one of the girls in our class.

Her back was turned to us. My friend was admiring the scenery and inviting me to join him. War was declared and there was a battle raging in my soul. Little soldiers ran toward one another with tiny firearms and bayonets. Miniature cannons shot off, and spiritual bombs were dropped. By God's grace, the good guys won—that time.

Instead of looking at her, I looked at my friend and said, "Nah, I'm good, man."

"What?" he said.

"I'd rather not look at her like that. I don't want to lust after her."

"Wow!" he exclaimed. "I'm a Christian, too, but why have you started to be so over the top lately? Why are you trying to be some kind of super-Christian?"

I can't count how many times I had conversations like that after the Lord began to change me. Some of those conversations were with people who didn't know me, but often they were with friends, sometimes even family. Apparently it was okay for me to like Jesus as long as I didn't get too serious and actually start to do what He said. Of course nobody would have said it that way, but that's how I began to feel.

I remember one conversation where a family member was frustrated with my preoccupation with the Bible. "Sometimes you can just do what you want to do," he said. "There's not an answer for *everything* in the Bible." I know the Bible doesn't say $1 + 1 = 2$, but it does tell me how to make decisions and interact with friends. Was I trying too hard?

In hindsight, I may have been young and annoying, but I don't think I was aiming for anything more than what God called me to. I don't mean that I was extraordinary or that the Lord called me to some special status as a super-Christian. I think He merely called me to do the same thing He calls all His people to do every day. There are no super-Christians, only regular Christians denying themselves and embracing their Lord.

SHOULD YOU CHANGE?

Over the years the music industry has given us numerous self-acceptance anthems, some with good messages and others with confusing messages. One of the most in-your-face of these anthems is one you might be familiar with. The catchy chorus, reminiscent of eighties pop music, says this: "Don't hide yourself in regret / Just love yourself and you're set."[1]

I never thought I'd be quoting Lady Gaga lyrics in a book, but they always grab my attention when I hear them. The sentiment in her hit "Born This Way" reflects the way so many of us think: "You're perfect just how you are, so don't try to change anything. Just embrace yourself." That sounds like a really uplifting message that many of us would love to hear.

It sounds like she's encouraging you to be content and be yourself, but she takes it a few steps too far, which makes the message deceitful. These lyrics assume if God made us, that must mean there's nothing wrong with us, but clearly that's not true. Have you looked at yourself and your friends lately? There are some things about us that need changing. God did create us, and He's never made any mistakes, but that doesn't mean we're all on the "right track."

The message feels nice when we hear it, because we like the freedom to ignore what everyone else thinks and do what feels right to us. We don't like trying to change ourselves. Everything would be much easier if we could just stay the way we are, but Jesus is going to encourage us to do the exact opposite. All of us can make the choice to do what we feel like all the time, but we have to realize that we cannot follow ourselves and follow Jesus at the same time. He was clear about that in His sermons.

Jesus said, "If anyone would come after me, let him deny himself and take up his cross" (Luke 9:23). That's not exactly the motivational message you'd hope to hear from such a famous teacher and leader. He wasn't saying, "If you want to follow Me, just be yourself." He was saying, "If you want to follow Me, it's going to hurt and you have to deny yourself." That means often saying no to yourself, refusing yourself, rejecting yourself. You probably wouldn't put that on a Hallmark card.

Is Jesus just being controlling and mean and insulting?

Why isn't He more tolerant? Because He can't be. And we wouldn't want Him to be. The last thing we should expect or want from Jesus is tolerance of our sin. He loves us too much to leave us in it, so He calls us out of it.

Of course, if we were perfect, asking us to deny ourselves would be ridiculous. If we were always good and wise, asking us to deny ourselves would be strange. But if we're flawed, asking us to deny ourselves is loving. If we're misled and messed up, asking us to deny ourselves is helpful. And we need the help.

THE NEED TO DENY OURSELVES

Have you ever realized how difficult it is to do what's right? It's not just you; it's all of us. God makes that pretty clear all through the Bible. One of the clearest places is in Psalm 53. If you ever want to know what God thinks of us, this psalm gives us part of that picture.

Verse 2 says, "God looks down from heaven on all mankind to see if there are any who understand, any who seek God" (NIV).

Have you ever been flying on a plane and as you land you look down below? You have a unique vantage point where you're able to see everything and take it all in. This verse gives us a picture of God's vantage point. Except His bird's-eye view isn't just of a neighborhood, or a city, or even a nation. He sees the entire world. And He doesn't just see people's tiny little bodies. He sees their hearts.

And as God looks, He searches to see if there are any righteous men, if there are any who have understanding or who actually seek Him, and what does He find? "Everyone has turned away, all have become corrupt; there is no one who does good, not even one" (Ps. 53:3 NIV).

Instead of finding people who seek Him, He finds people who are running in the other direction. Instead of finding people who have understanding, He finds people who are morally ruined. They're polluted with evil through and through. Like watching a drop of poison splash in a glass and declaring all the water undrinkable, God sees that all mankind has become corrupt. To say the least, God is not excited about what He sees.

The only time God looked down and found such a righteous man was when His Son was on this earth. We get to see this beautiful picture in Matthew 3: "And when Jesus was baptized, immediately he went up from the water, and behold, the heavens were opened to him, and he saw the Spirit of God descending like a dove and coming to rest on him; and behold, a voice from heaven said, 'This is my beloved Son, with whom I am well pleased'" (vv. 16–17).

The man who calls us to say no to self and yes to Him is the only man who's ever lived a perfectly righteous life.

If right before our wedding my wife had said, "To be my husband, you have to deny yourself and do everything I say," I may have had to leave her at the altar. If the president of the United States said it, I would move to France. If even my pastor said, "Deny yourself and do whatever I say, no matter what it is," I'd go to another church. Why? Because I don't want to let go of the wheel and let another sinner take complete control. That's ridiculous. They can't lead my life any more perfectly than I can, because they have their own set of issues.

But Jesus Christ is not another sinful person. He's holy, He's my Creator, and He died so sinners like me could be reconciled to God. He's trustworthy and He knows what my life should look like. He's not being mean; He's loving me.

It's loving of me to stop my son when he tries to put his finger in a socket or put a penny in his mouth. It's loving of Jesus to tell me to say no to myself when I'm doing the wrong thing. When you turn to follow Christ, you're agreeing to deny yourself; there's no way around it. And that goes for everyone. There is no caste system in the kingdom. All are saved by grace, and all have signed up to say no to themselves often.

Let's be clear, though. He's not saying you can't be yourself. He's not calling you to ignore your personality and abandon your interests. Instead, He's saying, "Submit all those things to Me." Your personality and your interests are His, and following Him shapes those things to bring you joy and bring God glory.

When was the last time you said no to yourself? Denying self isn't a one-time thing, but a daily task. Our hearts will always want to run in the other direction, but we have to say no. If you can't remember the last time you said no to yourself, you need to do some serious self-examination. I want to be painfully clear: Receiving Christ cannot be separated from denying self. Receiving Christ and denying self is looking at the same faith from a different angle.

I know this thought still sounds ridiculous to some, and I think I know why. We don't see Jesus as worth following.

JESUS IS NOT YOUR HOMEBOY

One of my favorite parts of each day is my son's bedtime. There is the selfish part of me that thinks, *Yes! Freedom from the tyranny of the toddler!* But what really makes this part of the day so special is that I get to read to my son. I've been waiting my whole life to use some of these special voices without people thinking I'm weird. My son is two years old, and this is my chance.

Lots of our family members have kindly purchased books for my little one, many of them Christian books that summarize Bible stories. Some of these books are amazing, and others are not so amazing. My biggest problem is often with the illustrations. They often make Jesus look like a weirdo.

I was looking through one of them and saw a picture of Jesus in a field with beautiful hair and a bunny on His shoulder, smiling while He played the ukulele. Are you kidding me? There are some things Scripture doesn't talk about, but I'm pretty sure my Lord did not play the ukulele or let rabbits sit on His shoulder like parrots.

That's an extreme example, but many of the other pictures

we get of Jesus aren't much better. He's weak, soft-spoken, and unable to defend Himself against Roman soldiers. I don't know who that guy is, but my Lord wasn't weak. In fact, He's the Almighty. When He was on earth, He told waves to calm down and they obeyed Him. Evil spirits threw tantrums when He showed up in their towns. He's the God-man, and He's worth following.

MORE THAN ANOTHER GUY

I remember the first time I heard Kanye and Jay-Z's *Watch the Throne* album. In one of the songs they made mention of Jesus, which may be exciting to some, but not to me. They listed some other historical figures like Malcolm X and Martin Luther King Jr., and then they mentioned their wives. They also mentioned Mary and Joseph. And then at the end of that list they threw in Jesus, baby Jesus to be specific.[2]

When I heard that, the first thing I thought was, *Those guys don't understand who Jesus is.* I'm not trying to judge their souls over what's in a rap album, but there's no way you could treat Jesus like just another guy if you knew who He was.

People constantly talk about Jesus as if He were just another good man and a good teacher. This couldn't be further from the truth, but people have been making this mistake for a long time. Jesus asked His disciples, "Who do people say the Son of Man is?" (Matt. 16:13 NIV). He was referring to Himself with that title.

The disciples had been around enough to hear what people were saying about their leader. I can imagine that as Jesus asked that question, different guys were chiming in with stuff they'd heard. They responded, "Some say John the Baptist; others say Elijah; and still others, Jeremiah or one of the prophets" (Matt. 16:14 NIV).

Now, you notice that no one responded with any negative views of Jesus. All the responses were positive, but none of them was really the correct response. Yes, all these men were honored, amazing, historic men of God. But none of them were who Jesus was. In fact, Jesus created those men!

When Jesus asked the disciples who they said He was, God revealed the correct answer to Peter: "You are the Christ, the Son of the living God" (Matt. 16:16). Jesus was way more than just some prophet or teacher. And to point to Him as anything less than the King of kings, the Lamb of God who takes away the sins of the world, is to reject Him and insult Him.

This is a King worth handing the keys of my life over to. Why wouldn't I deny myself for the opportunity to be led by Him? There's no one more trustworthy. There's never been a more humble servant or triumphant deliverer. So every day I choose again to get up and follow Him, and though it's never easy, He's always right. Real love doesn't overlook harm to make you feel better in the moment. Real love tells the truth even when it's hard. Jesus loves us too much to leave us where we are. And He died to take us to the Father.

CAN WE REALLY CHANGE?

"And I can't change / Even if I tried / Even if I wanted to."[3] Those are words from Macklemore's song "Same Love." All of us can relate to them because they ring true on one level. We cannot change ourselves. We are who we are. But that doesn't mean we can't *be* changed.

When we put our faith in Christ, God unleashes His great power toward us—the same power that raised Jesus from the grave. And that power is stronger than any lie the world tells us. Not only can every believer change, every believer *will* change.

There is no such thing as lower-class believers who never deny themselves, nor is there a grade of super-Christians who go above and beyond the ordinary by denying themselves. Denying yourself is part of what it means to follow Christ.

There are really only two ways to respond to Jesus: you can deny yourself and follow Him, or you can deny Him and follow yourself. Who do you think is the better leader?

• Part Two •

GROWING UP

5

TIME IS MONEY

I love Christmastime. When I was a kid it was mainly for selfish reasons. I wouldn't be able to sleep on Christmas Eve because I'd be hyped up on illegal doses of anticipation, fantasizing about action figures and Big Wheels. Somewhere in my late teens the action figures stopped pouring in, but I still looked forward to the season. These days I mostly look forward to giving gifts to others. I love the joy of figuring out what loved ones want and seeing the happy shock on their faces when they rip open a package.

I enjoy being generous. But my wonderful family, who happens to be especially generous, challenges that generous spirit every year. They all find great joy in lavishing one another with gifts. I benefit from the generosity, so I'm definitely not complaining.

The only problem is, when you give regular-level gifts, you feel like you did nothing. I gave one of my family members some books, knowing she loves reading, and while she was delighted to receive them, I felt like I had just handed her a trash bag. Not because she didn't show her gratitude, but because she took her generosity to a brand-new level that year.

She surprised the whole family when she handed envelopes to each of us that we had to open at the same time. I tore open the small cream envelope and discovered an ordinary Christmas card inside. I heard something swipe the ground, and when I realized a check had slipped out, I smiled and bent down to pick it up. Knowing her, I expected to see a generous sum, but this check was more than generous. It was huge. Not like a thousand dollars huge, but tens of thousands of dollars huge.

My first response was disbelief and then joy, then gratitude, then sobriety, and then borderline anxiety. That's a lot of money! I felt like I had been entrusted with a mammoth amount of cash, and I needed to think carefully about how to spend it. I didn't want to waste it.

I started to ask myself questions. *How much would I give to others? How much would I use to pay off debt? How much would I save? How much would I spend on myself?* It was a lot to think about, and I didn't want my aunt to think I was flippant about such a generous gift. My wife and I thought carefully and prayed earnestly about how to use this gift from a loving family member, but ultimately from God. We did our best to use it well.

The joyous, grateful weight we felt shouldn't be reserved for receiving huge monetary sums from family members, though. I want to talk about another generous gift that's been lavished on all of us, whether our families are wealthy, poor, or somewhere in between—that's the gift of time.

THE GIFT OF TIME

Most of us don't think of time as a gift. We just think of it as those twenty-four hours that seem to go by too fast. It's not something we think much about, except when we're watching the clock as we anticipate the end of our classes or workdays. Yes, we wish there were more hours in each day, but we know that's not how it works.

We usually think of time as something we have plenty of, especially when we're young. The important thing is that we try to get everything taken care of. We need to get that project done on time, pay those bills, or get that birthday gift sent out. Outside of that, we should just do what we want.

Scripture gives us a much different understanding of time. Scripture treats time less like an entitlement and more like a treasure. The Bible talks about time as if it's a loan from God that we should invest well. It's not like dirt, plentiful and worthless. It's like food, valuable and coveted by those who've run out. When we treat that diamond like dirt, we dishonor God and spit in the face of His generosity.

TIME INVESTORS

Many of you have probably heard of Bernie Madoff. He was a stockbroker and financial investor who started a wealth management business in the 1970s that was hugely successful. But today the name Madoff doesn't bring to mind brilliant investment strategies; it brings to mind fraud. He's currently in prison serving a sentence of 150 years.

His entire company was a scheme engineered to deceive his clients and make him rich. He had thousands of clients and squandered tens of billions of dollars. Some people lost their entire life savings by investing with Madoff.

Can you imagine entrusting someone with your money, expecting that he would help you invest it wisely, only to figure out you were being scammed? People were furious, and rightly so. Madoff was getting rich and they were getting tricked.

The money was never his to spend. His job was to use it for the investors' purposes, but instead he used it for his own. No one disputes the immorality of his actions. But while most of us would never think of acting like Madoff, of robbing another person of his life savings, we have no problem robbing God in a similar way.

Everything we have belongs to God, including our time.

We should invest it well, putting it where He tells us to instead of robbing Him and chasing what we think will satisfy us in the moment.

THE BEST USE

In his letter to the church at Ephesus, the apostle Paul told the church to walk wisely. And the first way he encouraged them to do that was by saying, "[Make] the best use of the time" (Eph. 5:16). He didn't say we should merely get things done; he said we should make the *best* use of the time. He encouraged the church to use this valuable resource to purchase good things. That's part of what it means to walk wisely in God's world.

Time management has always been a weak spot for me. I have an amazing and unique gift; I can convince myself to put anything off. I can lose track of time altogether, meandering off on various YouTube trails. Have you ever found yourself watching videos of squirrels slapping each other and asked yourself, *How did I get here?* Then you're like me. One thing always leads to another: I decide to check a quick e-mail, and I feel like I come out of an Internet coma an hour later.

Yet when people ask me about my time in God's Word, my first impulse is to tell them how busy I've been. It never seems like the right time for hard things, but it always seems like the right time for easy things. This has been a struggle for as long as I've had responsibilities. The Lord has helped me grow tremendously over the past few years, but this is still a daily fight. I actually wasted some time earlier today, knowing I needed to write this chapter on using time well. Why do I keep doing this?

WHY WE WASTE OUR TIME

One of our problems is that we think we belong to ourselves. Our assumption is that we are the masters of our lives and we get to make all the big decisions. That's a myth. I belong to God. First, because He created me (Ps. 139:13), and second, because He purchased me (1 Cor. 6:19–20). And that has serious implications for how I invest each hour of my day. I don't have the right to rob God of time.

My first job was as a cashier at a grocery store. I didn't always enjoy the job, but I loved getting that check every two weeks. If I worked a longer shift, I would get a break partway through. The break was only supposed to be thirty minutes, but I would always push the limit. Thirty-five or forty minutes one day, and if the managers were super busy I might even take fifty minutes or an hour. That was wrong of me to do, because I was getting paid for those hours. That grocery store bought those hours from me, and I was stealing from them.

God created us, purchased us, and put us to work. To ignore His purposes and treat our time like it belongs to us is to steal from Him. This isn't to say that we aren't allowed to do anything but pray and sing worship songs. But it does mean we should be thinking carefully about how to spend every moment for the glory of God.

Another problem we have is a distorted view of work and

other good things. I can look back on many times when I've procrastinated and not done things when I needed to. There have been times when I've allowed the evil one to deceive me about the nature of work. Work is a good thing. It's one of the ways we get to imitate God. But in my heart I've begun to believe that it's to be dreaded and avoided at all costs. That's what often leads to my procrastination, and I often have to fight that lie with the truth of Scripture.

WHY INVEST WELL?

Paul gave the Ephesians a reason to live carefully and make the most of their time that maybe isn't what you would expect. He said they should make the best use of the time because "the days are evil." That's a strange reason. What did he mean by that?

It seems to me that Paul was talking about the evil age we live in. We're fallen human beings living in a fallen world. We are to walk in wisdom and in light of God's will, and part of what that means is living as citizens of heaven in the here and now.

Most of the people around us in our neighborhoods, our campuses, or our workplaces don't know Christ. We're freed, but they remain enslaved to this evil world. Those of us who have been freed, then, should live differently among them. We should live wisely. Paul gave an example of what he meant a few verses later: we shouldn't be controlled by alcohol like so many are, but instead we should be controlled by the Spirit of God (Eph. 5:18). We should be aware of God's will to save through Christ and live lives that point people to Him in this evil world.

Not only that, but we have to look carefully at how we walk because our hearts will naturally drift away from God. We are easily distracted by so many things in this evil age. Our hearts are like dust particles floating in the air, and all it takes is a light breeze to blow them this way or that. Paul was saying, don't just go with the flow; pay careful attention to how you walk and be intentional with how you use your time. When we don't think about it, we won't use it well. It's that simple.

LIMITED TIME

I've never had a hallucination, but I can imagine it's frightening. Recently, I watched a TV show in which a man hallucinated about a friend who had died tragically a few years back. He knew the man wasn't there, but he saw him right in front of his face. And that led him to behave as if he were there. But just because the man saw his friend there, and acted like he was there, doesn't mean the friend was really there.

Young people hallucinate when it comes to time. We imagine that we have an infinite amount, when the exact opposite is true. We imagine that our time is like a mountain, standing firm, when in reality it's like a vapor, here now and gone soon.

Wasting time is insanity. It's like burning money. The

only difference is you can make more money, but you can never make more time. God gives you what God gives you. Not only that, but none of us know how much we've been given. There's no bank account we can check. There's not an iPhone app for that.

What if you had no idea how much money you had, and you weren't sure if you were dirt poor or if you were a millionaire? I bet you'd be careful how you spent every cent. You wouldn't waste money on expensive clothes or fancy vacations. You would only invest where it mattered.

Our time is like that. Who knows how much you have stored up in the bank? You may have fifty years left, or you may have five. This could be your last day. Don't hallucinate a stack of time in a vault. You get to make withdrawals every day, but you never know when your time card will get declined. You never know when the time machine will say "insufficient funds."

In addition, you don't know what will happen tomorrow. James rebuked the proud man who assumed he would do this or that tomorrow. He told him he should qualify all his plans with a humble posture that says, "If the Lord wills" (James 4:13–15). To put it simply, procrastination is pride, because it assumes you know the future. But we don't know when our health will decline or our lives will end. We don't even know for sure when life will get busier. Instead of presuming you'll have the time later, do what you need to do now. The only moment that's certain is the moment you're in. Every moment beyond that is a toss-up to us. Only God knows.

INVESTMENT TIPS

If time is money, how should you invest? The best strategy is to put your time into the things that will yield the greatest return; and since we're talking about time, the greatest return is eternal. You should invest your time in things that have an eternal impact.

You would never invest your life savings into a business if you knew it was going to fold by the end of the year. That would be insane. Why are we content to invest the majority of our time into things that are merely temporal?

Does investing time wisely mean you should spend every waking minute at your church's facilities studying Scripture? Should you quit your job to be a street preacher? For most of us, the answer to that question is no. Instead we should strive to be faithful where we are and do all things to the glory of God.

In short, you should spend your time loving God and loving others. It's a good idea to spend a Saturday afternoon helping a friend move or babysitting for young parents. Wouldn't it be great if you spent an evening reading through a few of the Minor Prophets? What if instead of watching every TV show on NBC on Monday nights, you used that night to get to know your neighbors, encouraging the believers and sharing with the skeptics? What if instead of surfing Facebook at your job or school, you actually did your work with excellence?

I like the phrase "time management" because it acknowledges that we are just managers of time, not the owners. We will have to answer to God for how we invest His time. What will we say? Think back to what you did this last week. How do you feel about answering to God for those things?

Sometimes we just waste our time, and other times we actually use it to sin against God. We should definitely not use the gift God gave us to rebel against Him. That would be like a wealthy friend giving you money and you using that money to take over her business. That would be betrayal! God has graciously given you time, so don't spend it dishonoring Him.

In Bible college, one of my professors assigned us a time journal. We were to journal everything we did with every fifteen-minute block of our lives. That was a devastating assignment for me. I wasted so much time! I spent so little time in the Word and prayer and so much time doing pretty much nothing.

I would encourage you to take part in this daunting task. It's like pulling up your banking statement and evaluating your spending habits. What do you typically do with morning hours? How much time do you waste with social media? Is it true that you don't have time to spend with others?

MAKE YOUR DAYS MATTER

I read a novel recently about a plague that killed all the men in the world except one. The last remaining man could no longer live the way he had before. The plague changed the way he thought about everything because he knew humanity's hope rested with him. Before the plague, he was just one among many, but now he was the only one left. Because of this, he recognized how significant his life was. But should it really take all that to change our minds? Are you significant even though you're one of many? Obviously, I think the answer to this question is yes.

Some may read this chapter and think: *This guy is taking life too seriously. He's the one who's hallucinating. Doesn't he realize how big this earth is and how little of an impact we really make? Instead, we should just use our little, puny lives to enjoy ourselves. He's right that we don't have a lot of time, so let's enjoy ourselves while we can.*

I read a comic strip that communicated something like this. It talked about how insignificant we are in light of the seven billion people on earth, and among all the people who have ever lived, and in light of the tiny galaxy we're in among the many, many galaxies. It sarcastically silenced young people who are zealous to make a difference in this world. The facts about population and the galaxies were true, but I hated the message it sent.

Let me be the one to inform you that every minute of your life has *huge* significance, your life along with those of the other seven billion people on earth. If you had been created to make the earth perfect, then you might as well quit because you never will do that. But if you were made for God's glory, then you matter.

Every second, every decision is a deposit into the bank of God's glory. All those deposits will be cashed in for praise on the last day. All God's people will rise from their seats and give the Lamb a standing ovation. And for eternity, those little decisions matter, because they contribute to the purpose for which everything was made. So get up, get out, and do something with your time.

You've been handed a huge check. What will you do with it?

6

HOME IMPROVEMENT

When I first got married, my flat-screen TV was usually tuned to *SportsCenter* or CNN. Somewhere along the way, HGTV—the channel about making your house cute—made it into the mix. Initially I watched some of the shows with my wife so I could make her watch basketball later, but eventually I started liking them.

The first show that grabbed my attention was called *Holmes on Homes*. Holmes is an expert contractor who knows everything about houses. In each episode, he would show up at someone's home and examine the problems they were having. The home was always much worse than they thought, and he would usually say something like, "Your house is in terrible shape and if you don't get out in five seconds, your whole family will die." Maybe they made it a little more dramatic for the entertainment value.

The confusing thing was that the homes always looked okay from the outside. But while watching the show, I learned that when homebuilders cut corners, disaster might be lurking even if everything looks fine. The roof may leak, wires may catch fire, and ceilings may even come crashing down. It's dangerous to build on shaky foundations.

Many of us have been trying to obey God and live good lives. Unfortunately, we've tried to do so while neglecting some foundational matters. And even though we appear to be just fine, we're poorly built and bound to collapse.

STAND ON FIRM GROUND

I've had plenty of Christian friends over the years. Some of them have had a deep understanding of the truth, and others have had a more shallow understanding. I've learned a lot from all of them. I want to tell you about three friends of mine in particular.

Friend number one attended church his whole life and even served in various ministries. Anyone looking at him from the outside would assume he was a Christian headed for heaven, but when I asked him what he based his salvation on, he timidly said, "My trials and tribulations." He didn't mention God's grace, the crucifixion, or even Jesus—even after I probed further. He was confident he was going to heaven, but he wasn't sure why he was so confident.

Let me tell you about a second friend. I overheard a conversation she was having one day after church. Sounding appalled, she said, "What?! The Holy Spirit's not a person! Where in the world did you get that from?" This argument went on for a while as a fellow church member slowly labored to show her what the Scriptures teach about Him. My friend had used the name "Holy Spirit" so many times in her life, yet she was still under the impression that He was just a force instead of the divine third person of the Trinity.

I want to introduce you to one more of my friends. He is a young man who had gone to church his whole life and served as part of his youth group before going to college. One day my phone rang, and he wanted to ask my opinion on something he'd been thinking about: "Do you have to speak in tongues to be saved?"

A church in his college town had taught him that speaking an unknown heavenly language was the only true evidence of knowing Jesus. It didn't sound right to him, but he had no firm basis for his disagreement. I was angered that a church would teach him something that's nowhere to be found in Scripture. And I longed for my friend to be firm in his beliefs about things as important as how we know we're saved.

Do you see a common theme in these stories? Each of my friends claimed Christ but didn't understand basic things about following Him, things like who He is and how He saves. They didn't think those issues were too important until life circumstances shook them up a bit. Sometimes it takes a spiritual earthquake for us to see things clearly.

My aim is not to pick at my friends. I'm using their examples because I think many of us will be able to relate. There was certainly a time in my life when I didn't understand very much about who God is and how He saves. I remember being confused by conflicting things I heard from different Christians I respected. I remember watching false teachers on TV and having no clue how dangerous they were. I had been born again, but I was a spiritual baby. My eyes had been opened, but I was still unsure about what I was looking at.

Does God mean for us to walk through life confused about who He is and how He works? Many of us claim to love God, yet we make little effort to go deeper with Him. None of us should be content with our current knowledge and understanding of the truth. Shallow roots lead to shaky footing, so if we want to stand firm we have to go deep.

STANDING IN THE STORM

Each of the three situations I described above began with tough conversations. Those interactions led my friends to do some serious soul searching, but sometimes life attacks us in more violent ways. I've seen it happen many times.

Not long ago a friend of mine lost his son. His one-year-old stopped breathing in the middle of the night, and his wife discovered their lifeless child after it was already too late. I still remember the moment I received that terrifying text message. I was frozen for a few minutes. My wife saw the terror in my eyes and reluctantly asked me what happened. I could barely mutter the words.

The news hit me hard because of my love for that family and their young boy. But it also seemed unbelievable because our sons were so close in age. I couldn't imagine losing my little man.

How are you supposed to respond when something so terrible happens? How do you keep from losing your mind? What are you going to cling to? What's to keep you from losing all hope? Did it happen because God is mad at you? Does God not love you anymore? Maybe God lost control for a minute? These are questions that will need to be answered.

My friends have been an amazing example of how to respond in such a difficult situation. It's not that they're superhumans with perfect character; it's that they know God and His perfect character. They'd been seeking Him, trying to obey Him, and studying His Word for years. They'd become intimately aware of His love and care for them. They'd read about His control over all things and His great wisdom.

If you were to ask them, they'd tell you the journey has been really tough. It's been the hardest season of their entire lives, and at times they've been close to despair. But they remain standing and trusting God in the midst of it.

There's no way you can be ready for such a terrible tragedy, but you can be prepared. They were prepared, because they knew their God. It certainly wasn't easy for them. But when the storm blew, they stood on solid ground. What about you?

GOING DEEP IN MY RELATIONSHIP

I want to go back to my own story for a moment. Early on as a Christian, I was content with my elementary understanding of God. I knew He was good, I knew He had a Son named Jesus, and I knew that I was going to heaven. What more did I need to know? But one day something life changing happened: I read God's Word and I tried to apply it the next day.

I don't remember what the exact passage was, but I remember it was something basic and practical from the book of James. I never would have denied that God's Word was relevant to real life, but I had never experienced it before then. The fact that something I read in the Bible actually applied to a real-life situation was truly eye opening, and it changed how I viewed God's Word going forward.

It was the first time I realized that God's Word is alive. This wasn't just some book full of wise sayings that I could take or leave. The living God of the universe had spoken to me, and He had a lot more to say. After that God gave me a deep desire to know Him in His Word. I had this new dissatisfaction with my own opinions. Instead of just knowing what I thought or what my parents thought or what the culture thought, I wanted to know what God thought. And His holy Word was the only place I could go to know for sure what He thought.

There are a few key moments in my Christian life where I can look back and see that God was at work in a special way. This was one of those moments. My newfound love for the words of God led to a much deeper love of God Himself. But couldn't I have gotten along just fine without this new love?

Many people have assumed that Christianity is merely an emotional exercise. To them, Christianity is about feeling and doing, not thinking. Others think that knowing a lot about the Bible is for pastors and scholars. Reading theology is for seminary students, not for everyday Christians.

One of the most important things I learned early on is that everyone is a theologian; some of us are good ones and others of us are bad ones. What I mean is that all of us have an understanding of who God is. Some have accurate pictures of Him, and others have inaccurate pictures.

Many of us have lived under the assumption that knowing the Bible well would be nice, but that it doesn't affect our relationship with God very much. This could not be more false. This would be like me saying I was no longer going to listen to my wife because, after all, I've already made a commitment to her and I do know her pretty well. Therefore there's nothing new I could learn about her that would have any real effect on our relationship. That's absurd, right?

Reading God's Word is an amazing relational interaction with Him. It's as personal and relational as a date night with my wife. The Holy Spirit of God wrote those words. Though Moses or the apostle Paul wasn't writing directly to me, the Holy Spirit wrote those words to me and to the original audience. Not only that, but the Holy Spirit is speaking to me through the Word as I read it. God Himself is talking to me. It's as if He's sitting across the table from me, leaning forward and looking me in the eye with an authoritative but loving stare.

Paul prayed that we would know the love of God, and we get that by going deep in His Word. Do you know what justification is? It's a glorious truth. What about election? Have you ever thought about what it means for God to be in control of every single thing that happens? What about the fact that He's everywhere at the same time? These are glorious truths that grow our love for God and deepen our commitment to Him.

PUTTING DOWN ROOTS

Psalms begins with an illustration that should encourage us to go deep. I could sum up the entire first psalm like this: blessed is the man who walks with God, because he will prosper; but cursed are those who oppose God, because they will perish.

I'll elaborate. Those who truly follow God are like a huge grand piano nailed to the floor; you can't move them if you try. On the other hand, those who oppose God are like a feather lying on the floor; all it takes is a good breeze to blow them away.

One of the characteristics of the righteous man is the role God's Word plays in his life. "His delight is in the law of the LORD, and on his law he meditates day and night" (Ps. 1:2). His delight and dedication to the Word of God are what strengthen his foundation and make him immovable.

It's not hard to imagine why a commitment to God's Word makes you sturdy. God's Word is eternal and unchanging. Our words, on the other hand, are not. Think about it. We purposely tell lies, and even when we're trying to be truthful, we're often terribly mistaken. On top of that, we change our minds from day to day. None of this is so with God.

His Word remains. He's never wrong, He doesn't change His mind, and He keeps all His promises. Isaiah 40:8 reminds us: "The grass withers, the flower fades, but the word of our God will stand forever." Standing on our own words is like trying to balance on a narrow balance beam. Standing on God's Word is like growing roots in the ground.

The moral of the story? Build your life on the Word of God. And I don't mean just declare that you think God's Word is true. I mean dedicate yourself to it. Meditate on it day and night. Do what God says. Building your life on the Word of God is an ongoing process, not a one-time thing.

GOING DEEP WITH MY ACTIONS

It's dangerous to do things without knowing why you do them. One of the reasons we often seem like we're fine is because we're doing all the "right things." But often we have no idea why we're doing those things.

You don't have to be a Christian to walk old ladies across

the street or feed the homeless. You don't have to know God in order to make sacrifices for your children. There are plenty of nonbelievers who decide not to live promiscuous or dishonest lifestyles. But when our reasons for doing these right things are shallow, it doesn't take much of a storm to wash them away.

This is part of why so many young people leave the church after they get into the real world. They never had any real, solid grounding. It's easy to stand still when you're inside during the storm, but when you step outside, the rules are different. The storms berate you and the winds try to knock you over.

Those winds may look like trials or false teaching, but they also often look like parties or serious doubts. I have friends who seemed to be following God when they left for college, but had altogether given up trying after their first year. If their foundations had been deeper, they would have found it much easier to withstand the bad weather. We have to find ways to push our roots deeper and deeper into the ground.

HELP FROM MY FRIENDS

One of the reasons I want to write books is because God has used books so much in my own life and growth. I remember when a friend of mine recommended I read *Knowing God* by J. I. Packer. I tore through that book and its words tore through my soul. I was never the same. I knew God was big, but that book helped me see Him in a much deeper way.

I know some of us don't like to read, but it's a habit worth cultivating. It can save your life. I've had difficult questions that I've found the answers to in good books. I've gone through dry seasons in my spiritual life, where I felt like I was slipping away, but God used books to pull me back in. Sometimes I don't even know what I need, but God speaks to me through a great Christian book.

I understand reading books is much different from reading the Bible. Reading the Bible is hearing from God. Reading books is more like talking to friends about what God said. Obviously hearing directly from God is more important, but that doesn't mean hearing from others is worthless. I don't know a lot of the people who wrote my favorite books, but I still consider them "friends."

I have "friends" who are pastors, scholars, and entrepreneurs. There are some I agree with a lot, and other friends I disagree with on some points but can still benefit from. Just like my regular friends, I'll take counsel when it's wise and biblical, and I'll go in another direction otherwise. Reading has been a huge part of my process of going deeper in God's truth. If you don't know where to start, ask someone you trust to point you in the right direction. But we can't stop at just reading what our friends have to say.

DEEP COMMUNITY

Of course, we can't ignore the role of God's people in our spiritual depth. Another key to going deep is finding a good church. You need to be a part of a community where the Word dwells deeply. You should build friendships with people who know Jesus better than you do. When I was about fifteen, I started to meet up with more mature Christians who opened up God's Word and helped me understand it better. It was an invaluable gift.

Not only that, but you should be sitting under good preaching. You should find a church where the pastor opens up the Bible, tells you what God said, and helps you think about how to respond. I don't mean where he reads a verse and then says whatever's on his mind. You want to hear preaching where the Scriptures are explained and applied, and where your face is in the text. Only after hearing deeply from the Word are we equipped to go out into the world to honor God.

Finding a good church should be one of your top priorities. In fact, before you choose a college or move for a new job, you should make sure you know of good churches in the area. The local church is necessary for our spiritual health, and we shouldn't overlook it for any job or university. Healthy foundations are key to a healthy spiritual life.

WHO AM I TO JUDGE?

Some may say I'm trying to intellectualize the faith and that I'm being spiritually arrogant. They say, "As long as people try to live good lives and obey what they do know, who are you to criticize them? After all, Christianity is about faith, not knowledge." That statement sounds nice and is even partly true.

Christianity, in a way unique from the world's other religions, is centered on faith. Each of our eternities hinges on whether or not we have faith. But faith does us no good if what we believe isn't true. God's Word informs our faith, and we should meditate on it day and night, that our faith would grow deeper. Many of us have been too content with a paraplegic faith instead of a strong, capable, active faith. Faith saves, but it also longs and progresses.

If we desire purity before God, Scripture tells us exactly how to maintain that: "How can a young man keep his way pure? By guarding it according to your word" (Ps. 119:9). It's not enough to skim Scripture; we need to know it well enough to guard our lives according to it. That requires real effort and intentionality. God meets us in His Word and rewards us with deeper knowledge of Him. Are you willing to prayerfully put in that effort?

The storms will come, and the world will try to pull us away. If we're going to follow Christ in this fallen world, we have to rise up, dig in, and go deep.

7

NOT GUILTY BY ASSOCIATION

One of my good friends takes me to the exact same place every time we have lunch together. He has a freakish loyalty to the place that I can't explain. It's very possible that he eats there for breakfast, lunch, and dinner seven days a week. I can't prove it, but I also can't disprove it since I've never seen him eat anywhere else. Part of it is intentional, so he can get to know the people who work there and share the gospel with them. But he also loves the food.

Over the years he's become a favorite among the employees. He's like the mayor of this place. When he walks up to the door, it's almost like his special theme music comes on and everyone in the restaurant is made aware of his presence. The door swings open on its own and the red carpet gets rolled out. And as he walks inside, hostesses, waiters, cooks, and busboys pop out from around every corner calling out, "Hey, Mark!"

The hostess hurries to take us to a booth—always the best one. And as we walk to the table, more people keep waving at him, welcoming him, and thanking him for gracing them with his presence once more. Young and old, rich and poor . . . okay, maybe I'm exaggerating a little bit. The point is: they love him there.

When we sit down, they already have the appetizers ready for us. They serve these delicious warm croissants with honey on them. They lay down a large plate with about fifteen of them. After we pray, that number dwindles quickly, but it's okay because the plate is always replenished. Before we even look at our menus, they already know his order. They say, "Rice and salmon with a Diet Coke, right?" He just smiles and nods his oversized head.

I'll admit the food at this restaurant is pretty good. But the experience becomes first class when you go there with him. You get treated with honor because you're with the guest of honor.

One time I was having lunch with another friend of mine, and I decided to take him to the same place. I had always had great experiences there with Mark, and I wanted to treat my friend to a great lunch.

I threw the door open, expecting to hear the amazing theme music, but instead—crickets. I was accustomed to a barrage of warm welcomes, but not this time. When I asked for a table, the hostess muttered lazily, "Uh . . . that's going to be like thirty minutes, man. Can you just sit over there in the corner for a second?"

Instead of being seated in the best booth, they threw us at a dusty table in the corner with spiderwebs and broken beer bottles on the ground. The floor under our table was sticky like an old movie theater with soda stains. And instead of a huge plate of fifteen croissants, we got a dirty plate with one and a half. Again, I may be exaggerating a bit, but let's just say I may never go there again without Mark.

The other times I'd been treated like the mayor because that's who I was with, but I had zero credibility when I went there on my own. The only way I get the royal treatment is when I'm with the one who's earned it. I can benefit only from his track record.

In God's sight, we've earned no credibility. Instead of first-class treatment, we've earned judgment. The only way we can be treated as sons of God is if we're associated with God's Son, united to Him by faith. In order to be received, we have to benefit from His track record, and that's exactly what God has available for us in Him. "For our sake he made him to be sin who knew no sin, so that in him we might become the righteousness of God" (2 Cor. 5:21).

That's really good news with really important implications. One of the most important is this: we have all the approval we'll ever need.

OUR PROBLEM

Have you ever looked at one of your own posts on social media—whether it's an angry rant or a picture of what you ate for breakfast—and checked to see how many likes, comments, or retweets you got? I'm sure most of us have at some point. If people responded positively to your post, it made you happy, but if it seemed like nobody noticed it, you were let down.

So we begin to shape our posts based on what will get the most responses. If our followers like deep quotes from theologians, then we'll dust off the C. S. Lewis book we've never read and search for something quotable. If our friends like to see pictures of us with cats, then we'll start harassing our neighbors in order to take pictures with their pets. Do you see what's happened? We no longer post things because we want to or because we should; we begin to post things in order to impress others.

The problem goes much deeper than social media, though. Often our desire for approval begins to rule different areas of our lives. How we treat other people, what we do with our free time, and even our moral decisions can begin to be ruled by what others think. Each moment turns into its own social media post, and our decision making is based on how many real-life likes we can get.

One of the problems with this is that it distorts everything. This obsession with others' approval has the potential to poison every thought we have, every decision we make, and every assessment of ourselves. It turns opportunities to glorify God into opportunities to glorify self. And when we begin fighting with God for glory, it never ends well. "I am the LORD; that is my name; my glory I give to no other" (Isa. 42:8).

Another problem with wanting everyone's approval is that we're longing after something we already have in much greater form. This is like Tiger Woods respecting my golf skills while I'm spending my time at Putt-Putt trying to impress the employees. God has already accepted us in Christ! And the beautiful thing is, it wasn't because of our performance, but because of His, so there's nothing we can do to mess it up.

But somehow that's not enough for us. We're dissatisfied with being embraced by the Creator of all things. Instead, we're in search of that magical feeling you get when another person approves of you or something you've done. We ignore our paid ransom in search of a pat on the back. This is insanity, but it's the reality for sinners like us.

Seeking approval from others is one of my biggest struggles, and it always has been. I'm a proud man. All of us are more or less proud, but it shows up in different ways. My pride struggle isn't thinking I'm amazing, but wanting everyone around me to think so. I'm well aware of all my flaws and shortcomings and weaknesses, but there's something in my heart that doesn't want anybody else to be aware of those things. Not only that, but I want them to be hyper-aware of all my strengths.

I can think of times when I've had interactions with people, and I find myself hours later replaying the conversation in my head and evaluating my performance. Sadly, the other person probably already forgot about it. I can think of times when I've done good things, not because they pleased God, but because I wanted to please people. And when my motivation is my glory instead of God's, that good deed is stained by my sinful posture.

As I write this chapter, I'm writing it to myself. I'm in it with you.

HOW IT SHOWS UP

This people-pleasing gene in our hearts shows up in different ways for each of us. We're especially susceptible to certain types of it during our high school and college years, because we're still establishing who we are and what we're about. For some of us there's this obsession with being popular or fitting in with certain groups.

If only we could see how temporary and unimportant that kind of acceptance is. Social popularity is fickle and temporary. But acceptance by God through Christ is rock solid and eternal. Of course there's nothing wrong with popularity, but it doesn't actually matter very much. That's easy to say in hindsight and sometimes hard to say when you're in the midst of it. But it helps to remember that the Most High accepts you and loves you, and He's brought you into His family—forever.

An uglier form of desiring popularity is when our desired friendships dictate our decision making. At the end of Kendrick Lamar's song "Peer Pressure," he says, "Usually I'm drug-free, but tonight I'm with the homies."[1] Haven't we all dealt with similar pressures? We allow our desire for approval to push us in directions we wouldn't go otherwise. The answer is to be more content with the acceptance of Jesus, while praying that God would make us more passionate about pleasing Him than pleasing other people.

This isn't something that goes away as we get older; we see parents, politicians, and public figures yielding to public opinion all the time. One of the quickest ways to ensure compromise is to obsess over what other people think of you. Sooner or later, the obsession with approval will make you do something that grieves God—all so you can please other people. If your main concern has been your glory all along, the decision to do that thing will be simple. You'll do what it takes to get it.

APPROVAL AMONG THE FAMILY

It's not just with the world that we feel this pressure for approval. Even among Christian friends we feel it. One of the ways this often shows up among believers is with the difficulty of openness and honesty about sin. Revealing the ugly corners of your soul is a scary thing, even when you know you should do it.

Have you ever been standing around at an informal gathering, maybe a party at a friend's house, and someone jumps to a serious conversation really quickly? You're standing there talking to a friend about football. "Man, I can't understand why he can't get it together! How many times can they lose like that? It's like they don't even want to—" All of a sudden you're interrupted.

"Hey, man! Have you been struggling with lust or anything lately?"

You think to yourself, *Whoa, man! Where did that come from?*

Then you have that strange battle in your soul. Of course the first thing that pops up in your heart is, *How dare this dude ask me that right now!* But then all those other emotions swim around in your heart a bit too. You know it's a good thing for people to ask you this, but really? Right now?

You know you should just respond and answer his question. But dang, there are so many people around. You have been struggling with lust quite a bit lately, but should you really leak that information right now in front of all these people? It would be more appropriate after church or at a small-group gathering. Or maybe even one-on-one at Starbucks.

You also don't want to seem lame. All these other people are Christians, too, and you don't want them to think you don't love God. You may struggle some, but you also live really Christlike in some ways. You'd rather give a more balanced perspective. You shared the gospel with your coworker or classmate recently. Why couldn't he have asked about that?

But you don't want to seem self-righteous either. All of us

struggle with something. You think, *How can I sound holy, but not too holy?* So without really thinking about it, you blurt out an answer, kind of. "Yeah, man, I am struggling with something. I've been, uh, praying way too much."

He looks at you, puzzled. "You pray too much?" You know that sounded stupid, but at this point you have to keep moving or you'll look even worse.

"Yeah, man, the Lord has really given me this desire to pray—for everyone. And I've been late for class and work. I know I should be a good steward of those things. So you know, pray that I'll, uh, pray less."

"Sure, man."

Now you evaluate yourself. *How did I do? Did I just blow it? I did. I'm such an idiot.* We've all been there, but why do we freeze up like that? Okay, it's a silly example. And many sins should be confessed in a more private setting. But why do we feel the need to pretend like everything's all right? Because we replace God's glory with our own, and we replace contentment in His acceptance with the approval of other people.

HUMILITY LEADS TO HEALTH

Recently I sat in a physician's office and talked with the doctor about a health issue I've had for a while. After she prescribed some new medications, she asked me a series of questions to make sure I was doing fine otherwise. I appreciated her inquiries, because she was trying to care for me as my doctor. If there had been something wrong, she could have acted immediately. The dumbest thing I could have done is hide my ailment from the very person appointed to help me with it.

Yet we're often tempted to make a similar mistake with our spiritual health. God has given us one another to help fight our sin, but we often hide from each other in shame. That's an understandable response for those who are still exposed and vulnerable to judgment. But our sin has already been covered, so we have no need to hide it. Why hide a bill that's already been paid?

Not only that, but hiding our sin is hazardous to our spiritual health. It's protecting our sin instead of fighting it. It's like creating a little greenhouse where we ensure that nothing will touch our sin and it will be able to grow. Instead we should want to expose our sin to everything that threatens it. Sin should be killed, not coddled.

As you read this, you may have some serious unconfessed sin in your life. Please remember this: Confession of sin is your friend, not your enemy. Confession of sin can only be perceived as your enemy if you have a goal other than God's glory. If your goal is your glory, then confessing your sin works against that goal and therefore should be avoided. But if you're living for the glory of God, confessing your sin to the right people will only help. Even when it hurts. But it's not easy to do. It takes humility, vulnerability, and sincere remorse.

Christians are, by definition, sinners saved by grace. If being Christians means we've already admitted we're not perfect, why do we pretend to be perfect for each other? It's like a whole hospital of patients telling one another they're not sick, all the while walking around with IVs in their arms. Jesus is our righteousness. Jesus came for sinners like you and me. We should feel free to confess our sins to others. It shouldn't be a revelation to anyone that we're messed-up sinners—all of us are.

SHOW'S OVER

We need to kill the disease in us that wants to perform for everyone. Putting on a show for others instead of being real doesn't help anybody. We've already talked about how it can hurt you, but what about others?

Non-Christians think we're hypocrites who are just as bad as they are but don't want to admit it. Instead of confirming their suspicions by hiding your sin, you should be honest. You are messed up and have issues. That gives you an opportunity to be clear about what you do with those issues. You give them to Jesus.

Christians struggle with insecurity about their spiritual state. When you pretend to be super holy, all it does is increase that insecurity in others. It fuels the lie they tell themselves, that they're the only ones who are this messed up. Instead of fueling that myth, you should be honest about your sin.

Every time I confess my sin to another Christian, he has some sin to confess to me as well. Confessing your sin encourages other Christians to do the same. And it reminds all of us of our need for Jesus.

With Christians or non-Christians, when we pretend, we are using them instead of loving them. Instead of saying or doing what would be most beneficial for them, we say or do what makes us look good. We're using them to get to that end goal, the magical feeling of acceptance and approval, that sweet ego stroke. And that will eventually crush us and crush them.

REST AND PEACE

When we go to spend an eternity with God, we will not be performing; we'll be resting. And we get to enjoy a foretaste of that rest right now! What does it look like for you to rest in Christ? It looks like trusting His righteousness instead of your own and building your life around that. What other people think doesn't matter much. That's a valuable peace to have.

Yes, people will make different types of judgments all throughout the day. Baristas will judge our drink orders and Christians will judge our knowledge of Scripture. But the judgment that matters most isn't today or tomorrow; it's the last day. And that judgment was taken care of at the cross. For those who trust in Christ, the verdict is "not guilty." We are sons and daughters, beloved by God. That should be enough.

Instead of trying to secure the approval of others, let's rest in the approval we already have. When you show up before God, you'll be with Jesus. And when you show up with Him, you get the first-class treatment He's earned for an eternity. Rest in it.

8

R&B

My first lessons about sex came from R&B albums. My father taught me many things about discipline, responsibility, and education, but R. Kelly and Dru Hill taught me about sex. Sometimes I'll hear an old song from the nineties (the golden era of R&B) and think, *Why in the world was I listening to this as a kid?* For example, on R. Kelly's first album, he actually had a song called "I Like the Crotch on You." I'll just leave it at that. Surely my parents had no idea what was spinning on my portable CD player.

It's hard to remember exactly what I thought about sex at that time. It may not have clicked with me that some of these songs were inappropriate for my young, moldable mind. I remember one time when my mom, my sister, and I were in the car and we played something we called the singing game. We would take turns singing a song during our drive to and from school or wherever we were going. There were no winners in this game, only losers, because we all had to stomach off-key renditions of popular songs.

My mom sang some old song by Phoebe Snow, and my sister probably sang Brandy's newest single. As they belted out their selections, I thought carefully about what song I should sing. I decided I would sing my new favorite song, "Nice and Slow" by Usher. I had gotten the CD recently, and I'd studied the lyrics from the booklet inside the jewel case. The first verse was going well until I got to a part about putting your hands in unseen places. My mom quickly stopped me and encouraged me to pick another song. I gave an awkward smile and sang a Michael Jackson song instead. I would pay money to go back in time and watch that moment.

Without even noticing it, sex had already become a part of my life. I watched sitcoms with sexual themes and story lines, and I inhaled music that described sexual interaction in imaginative detail. I had long ago stumbled upon late-night cable viewing, and I had been the willing victim of sensual pop-ups on the computer. And I know I'm not the only one.

Whether or not we seek them out, our eyes and ears are assaulted by sexual messages all day every day. Maybe you've been learning from romantic comedies or teen fiction, or maybe from TV shows and discussions over lunch. Our culture's insane obsession with sex has been in the air for some time now, and you can't help but inhale it. I'm starting to wonder if the pollution is permanent.

DRUNKEN LOVE

At the tail end of 2013, a historic event happened in the music industry. One of the biggest and most talented artists of our time released a surprise album. The LP was just over sixty minutes long and was self-titled *Beyoncé*.

I'll admit I was impressed by the hype she created by releasing it the way she did, not to mention the fact that there was a high-quality video for every song. I've never been a Beyoncé fan per se, but as an artist, I was very curious about this surprise work of art, as was my wife. So we checked it out. We were impressed by the music and taken aback by the content. The lyrics were overtly sexual and at times pornographic in their detail. I don't even want to mention the accompanying videos, most of which I had to cover my eyes for.

We were taken aback, not because sexuality seemed to be embraced and celebrated by a married woman, but because of the way it was celebrated. She didn't just express her love for her husband and affirm the goodness of sex, but she also exposed and flaunted her body for the world to see, in a way that should have been reserved for her husband. And it seemed like every song was like that. I don't recommend checking it out.

In my disbelief, I looked for reviews and commentary, thinking surely I wasn't the only one caught off guard. I figured there was somebody, somewhere, who appreciated the good-girl image Beyoncé had previously tried to uphold. Instead what I found was unrestrained praise. News outlets and feminist blogs applauded Beyoncé for finally being her true self and "owning her sexuality," thereby empowering women everywhere. They loved it.

That record sold more than eight hundred thousand units in the first few days, and well over a million in the first week. It made me cringe to think about the millions of young people who would inhale her project, appreciating the artistic excellence and ingesting this flawed message: that sexuality is merely yours to "own" and enjoy on your terms. I guess R&B strikes again.

CELEBRATE IT RIGHT

My view of sex is probably different from your average man in his midtwenties. Don't get me wrong, I see no problem with celebrating sex. In fact, I want to celebrate sex right now. Sex is an amazing gift from God Himself! Yay sex! Do you believe me?

I know sex is a good thing, and treating sex as a disgusting thing to be avoided is unacceptable. It's one of the greatest, most enjoyable gifts God has given us. My problem is the *way* the world celebrates sex.

Our world often treats sex as if it's the greatest thing life has to offer us. It puts an incredible amount of pressure on us to explore and experience everything we can as soon as we can. And they treat it like the experience is an end in itself.

While it is an amazing gift, sex is certainly not an end in itself. It's a glorious chapter of a much bigger and more glorious story. But by elevating it above everything else and separating it from its beautiful intended purposes, we actually lower its value and degrade it.

It's like spending all your money on furniture and forgetting to save anything for the house. When you don't have a house, furniture doesn't have much use anymore. It may be nice to sit in, and it may feel comfy, but you'll still be sitting in the streets with no permanent place to rest. So while you can obsess over furniture, you should probably rethink doing so. In the same way, obsessing over sex and forgetting its proper context is to lower the wonder of sex itself, and to remove its true beauty.

Some people reading this may think I'm a prude, but hear me out. It's not the biblical view that threatens your sexual fulfillment; it's the world's. If we're going to enjoy sex the way it was meant to be enjoyed, we have to rise above the world's low view and embrace sex the way it was *meant* to function.

WHAT'S THE PURPOSE OF SEX?

Many of us are accustomed to thinking of sex as something enjoyable, but we rarely think of it as something meaningful. We rarely think about our sexuality as something created by God to play a unique role in the story He's telling about Himself. But sex does indeed have such a purpose. Now I don't want to suggest that sex is the most important thing in the world, but I also don't want people to treat it like it's meaningless and stupid. Your sexual desires are not an accident. God gave them to you for a reason, and He intends to bring Himself glory through them.

If sex is about more than just personal pleasure between two consenting adults, what is it about? Sex is meant to be a physical expression of a greater reality: the coming together of a husband and wife in marriage. It's not that God only "lets" us have sex in marriage; it's that God created sex *for* marriage. We should not think of sex and marriage as different things, but one as part of the other. Just like studying is part of college, sex is part of marriage.

Sex is beautiful, but outside of marriage it loses everything that makes it that way. I'm not naive enough to suggest that sex outside of marriage feels bad. I'm not questioning whether it feels good; I'm asking if it *is* good. Sex is special, but when we pursue it outside of marriage it loses its meaning. While it should be a beautiful chapter in God's story, it's degraded to something ugly and foolish. From glorious storytelling to barbaric thrusting.

Not only that, but marriage itself is a symbol of an even greater reality: Christ's love for His church. Ephesians 5 tells us about that mystery. The depth of intimacy and joy felt in sex is only a small picture of the joy waiting for those who will be united with Christ for eternity. And thus the joy of sex is a means to the end of joy in Christ.

When we consider the glorious role marriage plays in God's world, it seems even more foolish for us to tarnish that picture. A lot is at stake, so we should think twice before treating sex like our servant instead of God's.

BUT I WANT TO!

I suspect that some of you are unconvinced by what I've said so far. None of my arguments change the fact we want sex and that most people enjoy it when they have it. Sex is desirable, so it's hard to stomach calls to avoid something that seems so obviously good.

I was talking to some high school students about sexual purity one afternoon, and they began to talk to me about how hard it was for them. They acted like it was somehow easy for me, but it's not! No matter how holy you are trying to be, no young person is immune from this desire. We all want it, and if we're going to be pure, it's not going to be easy for any of us. The question becomes, why would God give us these desires if we're not supposed to act on them?

Sexual desire is like ammunition in your weapon. It's a good thing if you use your weapon to defend the peace. But it's a bad thing if you use it for destruction. Lust is the same thing: sexual desire used, like ammunition, for an evil purpose. Sex outside of marriage is a perversion of God's gift. We are sinners, and our sinful hearts distort everything, including the great gift of sexual desire. Thus, lust is the horrible disfiguring of our sexual desires, turning a good man into a monster.

I watched a movie in which a group of psychologists did an experiment about the connection between despair and impatience. I know it sounds like a deep movie, but it definitely wasn't. Anyway, their experiment looked something like this: The psychologists would have subjects come into a room, and they would make them wait for the doctors to return shortly. A pink box of donuts sat on the table in front of the subjects. One of the psychologists would tell the subjects that those donuts were stale and some new ones would be right out. But some of the subjects couldn't wait. They chose to eat stale, hard donuts over waiting for fresh, soft ones. It was a fictional movie and a fictional experiment, but it sounds a lot like our battle with sex.

Why couldn't they wait? Didn't they trust what the people said? They may have believed that more donuts were coming, but they didn't believe that the fresh ones were worth the wait.

Sex seems incredibly desirable to us. It sits there in front of us, calling our names. We're told that we can wait, but we don't want to, because we don't believe God. You can allow impatience to lead you to the less God-glorifying sex, or you can trust God and wait. You can be patient, knowing that God will keep His Word. Sex within His context and parameters is best. Don't settle and sell yourself short.

WHY SAY NO?

Struggling with sexual purity is, of course, nothing new. Paul wrote to the Corinthians about their sexuality and what it meant (1 Cor. 6). He reminded them of four crucial truths that we, too, should keep in mind in our own battles for purity.

Who We're United To

Paul wrote, "Do you not know that your bodies are members of Christ?" (1 Cor. 6:15). One of Paul's main arguments was to remind them of a reality that was already present. Not only did they belong to Jesus, but they were also one with Jesus. He calls us His body. We're not *a* body of Christ, but *the* body of Christ. We function as an extension of His presence in His world, not just spiritually but also physically.

That has amazing implications. Listen to Paul again in the same verse: "Shall I then take the members of Christ and make them members of a prostitute? Never!" Wow. This is strong and graphic language. He's saying your body is part of Christ's body, so how dare you use one of Jesus' body parts to sin against Him? Jesus would never have engaged in sexual immorality, so how dare we involve Him in such evil?

Has it ever occurred to you that this is what we do when

we engage in sexual immorality? We not only offend Jesus with our mess, but we drag Him into it. Someone who is one spirit with the Lord has no business becoming one flesh with anyone who's not his or her spouse.

What Sex Is

Paul reminded the Corinthians of part of the big picture we've already talked about: sex is meant to further illustrate and maintain the reality of coming together in marriage. Husband and wife are one flesh, and sex illustrates and further accomplishes that. What sense does it make to do this with someone who's not your spouse?

"Or do you not know that he who is joined to a prostitute becomes one body with her? For, as it is written, 'The two will become one flesh'" (1 Cor. 6:16). (Don't get too caught up with the word *prostitute* in the passage. Paul's emphasis wasn't on the person's profession, but on whether or not the person is your spouse.) Paul was quoting Genesis 2 in those verses, where God introduced marriage into the picture. And this amazing act we've degraded is meant to illustrate that beautiful gift.

I'll try to make this point without getting graphic. It is impossible to be more closely connected to someone than when you're having sexual intercourse. There is a literal oneness that occurs.

Marriage is giving of yourself in every way. And this physical giving of yourself, recognizing that your body belongs to your spouse because you are one, isn't meant to happen with boyfriends and girlfriends. Nor with prostitutes or one-night stands.

The union of man and wife communicates something special about the union between God and man. When we mess with that and become one flesh physically with different people, we lie about the gospel. Lying down with your boyfriend or girlfriend is lying about Jesus. Marriage is a masterful illustration, and when we have sex outside of marriage, we're messing with the clearest picture He's imbedded into creation of His love for His people. Marriage is a parable we get to take part in, so a lot is at stake with your purity.

What Our Bodies Are For

It seems that some of the Corinthians imagined that God wasn't so concerned about their physical bodies, and Paul wanted to set that straight. God created our whole beings, purchased our whole beings, and cares about our whole beings. Do you ever imagine that as long as you go to church and pray, God is fine with your lifestyle? That maybe He doesn't like that you have sex outside marriage, but what's important is that you do all the spiritual stuff?

If you think that, you couldn't be further from the truth. Here is Paul in the same passage: "Flee from sexual immorality. Every other sin a person commits is outside the body, but the sexually immoral person sins against his own body" (1 Cor. 6:18). God intends to use even our physical bodies for His glory. We will spend eternity in physical bodies worshipping our Lord. God cares about what we do with them. We are to honor Him with them.

"The body is not meant for sexual immorality, but for the Lord, and the Lord for the body. . . . Glorify God in your body" (1 Cor. 6:13, 20). Honoring your body doesn't mean not having sex at all; rather, it means allowing sex to play its proper role. It means not becoming one flesh with people you're not united to in marriage.

Whose We Are

The reason you should honor God in your body is this: "for you were bought with a price" (1 Cor. 6:20). We're not our own, but God's. Wouldn't you be devastated if someone used your belongings to do horrible evil? Let's not use our blood-bought bodies to rebel against the Lord who died to redeem them.

WHAT IF I ALREADY MESSED UP?

Scripture is abundantly clear about how the believer should view sex. There's no ambiguity about the role sex should play in our lives. But what if it's too late for some of us?

I'll be honest with you. I wasn't sexually pure before I got married. Before I met my wife, I dishonored God with some of the relationships I had. And I looked at things I never should have looked at.

On my wedding night I was grieved that my wife had remained pure while I hadn't. I was hurt that I couldn't give her what she was giving me. How did I deal with it? I didn't implode with guilt or keep thinking about it. Instead I remembered what Christ had already done with my sin. Jesus died even for sexual sin, and He makes all things new.

If you've already messed up, confess that sin to God and turn away from it from now on. Don't pretend it's nothing, but don't imagine that you're worthless or damaged goods. God is a powerful redeemer, and He can even use our past mistakes to tell His great story.

Every now and then I'll turn on the radio as I drive around DC, and there will be some new R&B song on. The songs are just as raunchy as they were when I was growing up, but I'm different. I know what sex is about now. It's not just about my experience or owning my own sexuality. It's about God.

R&B is constantly lifting up sex, but in its obsession, R&B has actually done the reverse. By making it mean everything, they've made it mean nothing, and that's a tragic waste of a great gift. Only in Christ can our sexuality rise back into its proper place.

9

DON'T DRINK THE KOOL-AID

The story of Jim Jones and the destruction he caused is one of the most devastating stories I've ever heard. Maybe you've heard the story before. Jones was a Communist and a false teacher who pretended to be a Christian pastor for many years. He led a cult known as the "Peoples Temple" and taught strange things, such as married couples abstaining from sex and only adopting children. Like all cult leaders, he was very controlling over those who chose to join the community he'd built. He was like a bad shepherd, making sure sheep stayed in danger rather than escaping.

All false teaching is dangerous, but Jones's leadership proved to be deadly in more than one sense of the word. The community continued to grow, and eventually the surrounding world began to learn more about the abusive practices at the Peoples Temple. A congressman went to Jonestown to investigate. That didn't end well.

The congressman was murdered along with four others; and after that happened, Jones knew that his run was over. He convinced his followers that the government would descend upon their community and murder and torture their children, so it would be better to drink poison than to face the coming punishment. More than nine hundred people, including three hundred children, died that day in a tragic, murderous mass suicide.

Real people were deceived into drinking real poison and giving it to their children. And the saddest part is that many were manipulated into drinking it willingly. They had been brainwashed by a delusional man who, after feeding them lies for years, encouraged them to wash those lies down with a deadly cocktail. They drank the "Kool-Aid," knowing the contents were polluted, but believing that the outcome would be best.

It may be hard for us to imagine being so deceived that we would willingly ingest something so deadly. But a devastating number of us do it all the time. In fact, our deadly potion of choice has become something of an epidemic, destroying an unimaginable number of people. Our generation's sin-spiked Kool-Aid is pornography.

We've been tricked too. We willingly drink it in, knowing it's wrong but falsely believing it's something to be desired. The act is wicked and the result is deadly, but our culture doesn't seem to understand that.

IS IT THAT BAD?

I realize the Jonestown tragedy is a weighty story to begin a chapter with, but I don't bring it to your attention lightly. I would never belittle that tragedy in an attempt to shock you into finishing my book (though you should definitely finish my book). I want you to grasp the deadly nature of porn. We get tricked into thinking it's our friend, but it's not.

Many may think it's ridiculous to compare something like staring at a few pictures or videos to drinking lethal poison, but I don't think the connection is farfetched. You may survive physically, but each time you view porn, you're draining life from your soul.

I've heard many refer to us as "the porn generation," and others talk about the "pornification" of our country. You can word it however you wish, but there's no doubt that we have a porn problem. And I don't mean just guys. I don't want to say anything that reinforces the lie that this is just a male problem. It may be more common for guys, but it's not rare for women. There are many women who struggle with porn, and the more we pretend it's only a male problem, the less women feel comfortable talking about it.

This is an everyone problem. It seems to have affected

all of us. It's rare to meet someone who hasn't been touched by its devastating effects. And I'm not just speaking about the nonbelieving world. This is a dark struggle for many Christians. The difference has to be that we fight. And our God has given us the power to do so.

REJECTING THE GAME PLAN

We shouldn't belittle the wickedness of embracing lustful activity. When you look at porn, you're rejecting God and His plan. You're saying, "God, I know this person is not my spouse and I'm not meant to look at them with lust, but I refuse to accept that. I will look at them this way, whether You like it or not." That's a bold and dangerous statement to make.

At the root of our porn problem is discontentment with God's plan for our sexuality. We don't trust God. We think He got it wrong. We don't like what He has to offer us, or at least His timing, so we go off in search of something else. Let's call porn consumption what it is: an attack on God's wisdom and an attempt to satisfy yourself apart from the One who created satisfaction and the One who ultimately satisfies. Searching for pleasure outside of what God provides is not a pattern you want to embrace.

REAP WHAT YOU SOW

Many people assume that porn is harmful but that they'll be freed from it when they finally do marry. Their sexual desires will be fulfilled and looking at porn will be a thing of the past. That's naive and, to be blunt, stupid. Building habits of sexual sin is not something that can just be turned off easily after you say your vows. We shouldn't imagine that the monster lurking in your soul will go dormant the minute you kiss your bride or groom.

Instead, you've sowed the seeds of sexual discontentment. You've built a habit of denying God's sexual plans for your own. And you can bet that discontentment will still be there after marriage. You'll still have to fight hard to put it to death. The longer you indulge it, the harder it will be to defeat. And sexual discontentment often leads to other kinds of marital unfaithfulness. This is not something to be played with.

If you've imagined porn isn't that bad because it's not actual intercourse, you should get rid of that thought right away. Don't live under the illusion that you can enjoy sexual intimacy while still abstaining from sex. All sexual immorality is sinful. All lust is offensive to God. If it turns you on, you should turn it off.

Many of us run to porn because it's something that feels good in the midst of a life where nothing seems to go right, whether our jobs or our marriages or other relationships. But there is no real comfort to be found in porn. Like alcohol, the intoxicating effects may make us forget our problems for a moment, but after the feeling wears off, we're left in a worse situation than before.

Others of us fall in times of idleness. Boredom leads to aimless surfing, which leads to curiosity, and so on. Or maybe you've built such a habit that you hate it but can't stop. You intentionally go searching for wicked images several times a day. Maybe you wonder if you're addicted. Whatever your situation, you should take the fight seriously.

WHAT'S SO BAD ABOUT IT?

I keep saying porn is destructive, but am I just overreacting? No. Here are three ways it wreaks havoc in our lives.

Porn pulls us away from God

When we choose wicked images over God, we're pulling ourselves farther and farther away from Him. Imagine you are in prison and can only talk to your loved ones on an old phone through a glass wall. It's not that God won't hear you when you speak to Him, but there will be a wedge between you. There's intimacy that you cannot have with God while chasing after counterfeit intimacy with men or women on computer screens.

For every moment you seek your satisfaction elsewhere, you will not be seeking it in God.

Porn gives us a distorted view of the opposite sex

Those people whose bodies are captured in images on your computer screen or smartphone are made in the image of God. You're objectifying them. You're insulting God. You're treating His image with disdain and perversion.

You're supporting an evil industry that destroys lives and

marriages. You're supporting an industry that is known to enslave and manipulate young women. Instead of caring for the weak, hurting, and confused, you're supporting their pain and confusion. You're encouraging them in it. With each click, you're giving it a thumbs-up. Instead of seeing them how God sees them, you're looking at them through broken lenses.

Porn doesn't just affect the way you see the participants; it distorts the way you see everyone. Porn has a way of distorting your worldview. If you spend your time indulging in porn, looking at all sorts of people naked and objectifying them regularly, do you imagine you'll be able to turn that off when you go into the real world? Do you imagine you'll be able to turn that off when you go to church?

You're training yourself to look at other people in the wrong way, and your heart and mind will respond to your training regimen. Indulging in porn undercuts your ability to love others as you've been called to.

Porn hinders enjoyment of real intimacy

Porn gives us a faulty view of sex. Not only because we're seeking to enjoy sexual pleasure of different types apart from marriage, but also because it's like a movie (if you can even call it that). Cops in movies jump from rooftop to rooftop and fly through the air gracefully as a car explodes behind them. But we should not expect the same from real cops.

Porn is just as fake. There is often nothing real about what you're looking at, so we should not expect our sex lives to be like porn. Yet, when we indulge in it, we train ourselves to think of sex in a particular way. But by the very nature of the medium, we're training ourselves in something fake.

Not only that, but you're hurting your intimacy with your present or future spouse. All your sexual desires are to be aimed toward him or her. And you'll have to redirect them. There are certain images that will never leave your mind, and this is one of the devastating consequences of this sin.

DEFENSE

I wanted to spend the majority of this chapter impressing upon you the danger and wickedness of porn. I did that because the most important thing in your fight against porn is that you see it as the despicable enemy it is. Until we see how ugly porn is, we won't fight it with all we have. When I play games with my son, I go easy on him because he could never win. He's a playful opponent. But if I'm going against a threat, I need to be in attack mode. Brothers and sisters, we need to be in attack mode.

We need to do drastic things. Jesus talked about plucking out our eyes and cutting off our limbs, because the stakes are that high with sin. Porn is no exception. Some of us need to delete our social media apps because idle clicking always leads to the same place. We need to tell our friends all our dirt. We need to get accountability software. We need to get rid of our laptops and phones. Are you willing to do the drastic things you need to do?

What about guarding yourself while you're doing

regular things? Know what leads your mind in the wrong direction and stay away. Don't expect that if you exercise no self-control with your eyes when you're out that you will when you're home. Build habits of self-control. Fast-forward through those scenes that cause you to stumble. Be willing to walk out of a movie.

There is no halfway or lackadaisical way to fight lust. If you're not fighting your sin, you're befriending your sin.

We need to pursue practical ways to fight off our sin, but more than any of these other tactics, we need to look to Christ. He is greater than porn. And until we understand that, we'll keep settling for the spiked Kool-Aid.

10

WHY I GOT MARRIED YOUNG

On a late-night stop at the store to grab a few things, I had a conversation with the cashier. We made small talk as she scanned my items, and then she offered me a discount card. I told her my wife already had one, and that's when things got fun. I know this conversation all too well because I've had it many times before. It goes something like this:

PERSON: What? You're married?

ME: Yeah, I've been married for several years now. It's amazing.

PERSON: How old are you? You look like a baby.

ME: Midtwenties.

PERSON: You're so young! Why in the world would
you do such a thing?

ME: Why wouldn't I?

In 2009, I got married at the barely legal and barely
respectable age of twenty-one. During my courtship, engagement, and marriage, I've been asked time and time again,
"Why get married so young? What's the rush?" And my personal favorite: "You should have waited and enjoyed your life!"

Some of the folks asking these questions were strangers,
but some were family. Was I crazy to get married at such a
"young" age? Here are the reasons why I got married young.

I met a godly woman

As an eighteen-year-old freshman in Bible college, I wasn't
actively looking for a wife. I wasn't surfing Christian Mingle
or looking through the yearbook for pretty faces; I was just
minding my own business. But God saw fit to introduce me
to a girl named Jessica. I was excited to get to know her, and
eventually I wanted to date her.

I was ready

By this time I began to think about the reality of marriage and what it means to commit yourself to someone for
a lifetime. I asked myself whether or not I was mature and
responsible enough. I searched through the Scriptures and

thought about the responsibilities of a husband, and I talked to married friends and mentors.

After lots of prayer and conversation, my mentors and the pastors in my church told me they thought I was ready to pursue her. I was elated. But I wouldn't have pursued her if I thought I wasn't prepared to spiritually lead her, provide for her, and be the head of a family.

Marriage is a blessing

At first I felt like I had to prove to the naysayers that getting married young is okay sometimes. When I looked in the Scriptures, I didn't find stuff like, "Marriage equals death! Flee from it!" or "Put marriage off until you can't put it off any longer" or "Only get married when you're too old to enjoy life" or "Play the field for a while and then pick the best one."

Instead I found commands like "Flee youthful lust" and I read passages like Proverbs 18:22: "He who finds a wife finds a good thing and obtains favor from the LORD."

So when people ask, "What possessed you to get married so young?" my new response is, "You're asking the wrong question." I think at the root of that question is the assumption that marriage steals something away from us, as if youth is wasted in committed, sacrificial love when it could be used for casual pleasure and flakiness.

Marriage is a beautiful gift from God! It is a means of grace. I found a wife, and that is a good thing. I don't agree with the logic that says to put off God's richest blessings as long as you can. Instead I would say enjoy God's good gifts and steward them for His glory.

NO REGRETS

Often people will ask me if I regret getting married so young. My answer? Absolutely not. It's one of the best decisions I ever made. I'm happier and holier than I was in 2008, and that's a good thing. And I don't want to make it seem like I'm some super-rare anomaly. I know plenty of folks who got married just as young or younger than I did. They, too, saw marriage as a gift, and they've seen the fruit of that gift. My wife and I may be young now, but I'm praying for grace to love her well until the end of our lives. Until then I want to obey the wisdom of Proverbs and "rejoice in the wife of [my] youth" (5:18 NIV).

CHOOSING A SPOUSE

Whenever I post pictures of my family on social media, the responses are always fun. The most common are, "Your son is so handsome!" or "What a beautiful family!" But one of the other common responses is, "Is your wife white?" People ask me at shows sometimes too. The answer is yes. My wife is a mix of Hungarian, Italian, and Polish—which to most people just means, yes, she's white. This is irrelevant to some, but shocking or even disappointing to others. I don't think anyone should be shocked or disappointed by interracial marriages, but I still want to talk about why I married "outside my race."

The decision to marry someone from a different ethnic background wasn't a tough one for me. I never sat down and wrote out a pros and cons list. Though if I did, the fact that my wife has never seen an episode of *Martin* would be in the con category. But honestly, I didn't agonize over it or seek counsel about whether it was okay. I was convinced that she was the woman for me to marry, even though she wasn't black.

Some would never consider marrying someone who isn't the same ethnicity as them, so let me tell you why I did.

EXPECTATIONS

To be honest, I always expected to marry a black woman. I found women of all backgrounds beautiful, but black girls were my "preference." When I arrived on my college campus in 2006, I wasn't looking for a wife at all. I just wanted to grow in my faith and get a good education. My first album had just come out, so I had plenty of other things to focus on. But as I met people at the school, a sophomore named Jessica really caught my attention and we became friends.

We ran in the same circles and we ended up joining the same church, so we saw each other a lot. And the more I got to know her, the more I was drawn to her. She really loved Jesus, and she had this childlike willingness to do whatever He asked. Her compassion for needy people challenged me, and she had a humble heart that responded to the Word.

During that first year, I watched her sacrifice countless hours of her time serving at our church. On top of all that, I loved being around her. Our conversations, whether serious or silly, always flowed with ease. I eventually started to ask myself, *Should I marry this girl?*

PREFERENCES

Jessica didn't look like I expected my future wife to look, but honestly, that didn't matter to me. Don't get me wrong. I thought she was beautiful from the first time I met her. And I was never opposed to marrying a white girl. I just didn't think I would. But as I grew in my faith and my heart changed, my preferences started changing too. My main preference was that my wife be godly, and Jessica was. So I wifed her.

Never for a moment did I feel like I was settling. It feels more like settling to overlook a godly woman merely because of her ethnicity. I never wanted to value my preferences for a wife over what I needed in a wife.

There's nothing necessarily wrong with having preferences, but we have to hold them with an open hand. I know some people who overlook a potential godly spouse because the person doesn't fit some random preference. Some of our preferences really don't matter that much. Some of our preferences may even be foolish. We have to submit all of them to Scripture.

When you and your spouse are in the middle of conflict, skin tone doesn't matter. Body type and social status seem insignificant. At that moment you want the person to be godly and humble. And as my wife and I began to raise our first child, I couldn't have been more grateful for her. She's an amazing mom and a godly influence on our children—neither of which have anything to do with her ethnic background. It's okay to want things in a spouse, but we have to submit our desires to what God wants for us in a spouse. What I wanted and needed most was a godly partner, and that's exactly what God provided.

SHOULD YOU GET MARRIED YOUNG?

The purpose of this chapter is not to convince you to get married tomorrow. I'm not saying everyone should get married when I did. It would have gone badly if I had tried to get married before I was ready. Some of us do need to mature more, and others of us need to pray for contentment and trust the Lord and His timing. My goal is not to say that the younger you get married, the more holy you are. I just want to dispel the myth that we should delay adulthood and only consider marriage after we're thirty or older. Whatever age you are, seek to view marriage the way God does.

If marriage were a book and asked me for an endorsement, my blurb on the back of the book would be pretty simple: "Marriage is amazing. I highly recommend it."

11

AGE IS MORE THAN JUST A NUMBER

You've probably heard someone say it before. Maybe they were trying to explain why their newest love interest was so young, or maybe they just wanted some respect from their parents' generation. Whatever the scenario, the pithy statement "Age ain't nothing but a number" is a sure way to eliminate any ageism in the vicinity.

I agree that age doesn't equal maturity and youthfulness

doesn't equal stupidity. There's no question about that. Scripture speaks to this truth where the psalmist wrote: "I have more understanding than all my teachers" (Ps. 119:99). It's God's Word that brings wisdom, not mere age or position. While that should encourage us to seek wisdom in God's Word, it should not lead us to ignore the truth about age.

Age is indeed much more than just a number; it's a number that represents time. With time comes experience, and when experience connects with truth from God's Word, we get a unique brand of wisdom. Wisdom is more valuable than silver and gold, so we should value those who have it, and earnestly seek it out.

The problem is, our culture doesn't value age very much. We value cool, thin, and pretty, none of which are usually associated with old age. We run from old age like from a perp in the streets, but noticing we can't outrun it, we try to slow it down and pretend.

Watch TV for an evening, and you'll likely see ads about revolutionary creams that hide facial wrinkles or commercials that promise your life will improve if you'll buy some dye and hide those greys. Makeup artists smooth out rough skin, and magazines photoshop all signs of aging. Wrinkles and greys aren't beautiful to us. Our idea of beauty has excluded those whose bodies age naturally.

But what's wrong with age? I'm actually looking forward to it. I've noticed that when people get old they go one of two ways: they become either a really sweet old person or an extremely grumpy old person. I'm pretty sure I'll be on the grumpy side, but that's okay, because after a certain age you can say whatever you want and somehow it's okay. There are benefits!

Sure, I'm not looking forward to my body deteriorating, but I don't see age as anything to run from. There's a lot to be gained. In the meantime, I want to receive the wisdom God has given my older brothers and sisters in Christ. Because if I'm honest, I know I'm wrong about a lot of stuff, and sometimes I need more experienced eyes to help me see that.

A CALL FOR HUMILITY

While being younger doesn't mean we're dumber, it does mean we're inexperienced. Some of us have experienced a lot at a young age, but most of us have a lot of life we haven't seen yet. Maybe we're not married yet, or we've never been parents, and we've certainly never been laid off from a job we held for twenty years.

This inexperience should lead us to humility. Sure, no one knows everything, so everyone should be humble, but our inexperience should humble us even further. There are so many things we haven't seen yet, and for many of us our brains are still developing. There's nothing wrong with that, but we should be aware. Our youth should lead us to listen more than we talk and to posture ourselves as learners more often than teachers. We should sit at the feet of those who've already been where we're going.

I used to hate it when my dad would say things like,

"You'll understand it one day." He may have been referring to why I had to clean up my room, or why he wouldn't let me drive late at night, or why I couldn't put rims on my Nissan. It drove me crazy, but most of the time he was right.

There were so many things I didn't understand then that I do understand now. And I'm sure as I get older, lessons he taught me as a child will continue to click. If he were still here, he'd be glad to say, "I told you so, boy." It's not because I didn't trust him, but because I had some maturing to do. When I look at my crew of friends, I make sure a couple of old guys are there.

MY OLD FRIENDS

I've never been one of those guys who has a million close friends. I'm an introvert, and I can only handle so many friends at a time before my body crashes and I'm forced to escape to a remote location. I love being with people—as long as by people you mean a few people I know really well. I have to be very intentional with my friendships and the people I engage with, because I have less relational energy to spend.

Most of my close friends are just a little older than I am, but a couple of them are twice my age. One of my older friends has been a blessing to me for the past few years, and he's demonstrated a lot of humility by putting up with my old-person jokes. I have the spiritual gift of old-guy jokes, and he does old-guy stuff that begs to be made fun of. He's only in his fifties, but he already has that grumpy-old-man persona, in a godly way. Sometimes you need someone grumpy to tell it how it is, even if it's ugly. That would be my friend Matt.

He also happens to be white. I want you to imagine the scene as we walk down the street, headed to grab lunch or a quick coffee. People are so confused. Why is that fifty-year-old white man walking around with that fifteen-year-old black kid (apparently I look like a child to some people)? We get strange looks because people can't figure out why in the world we're friends. And to be honest, sometimes I ask myself that same question. How did we end up such good friends?

If we weren't Christians, we may never have spent enough time together to get close and enjoy each other's company. But he's one of the friends I appreciate most, because God has constantly answered my prayers for wisdom through him.

GO GET WISDOM

Have you ever read the book of Proverbs? It's filled with calls to flee foolishness and chase after wisdom. Here's one example: "The fear of the LORD is the beginning of knowledge, but fools despise wisdom and instruction" (Prov. 1:7 NIV). One such fool was a man named Rehoboam, whom we read about in the Old Testament.

Rehoboam was king and ironically the son of Solomon, a man known for his great wisdom. Rehoboam had a tough decision to make, and Scripture says first he "took counsel with the old men," men who had worked alongside his wise father (1 Kings 12:6). They wisely encouraged him to be good to the people, but Rehoboam didn't like their counsel. "But he abandoned the counsel that the old men gave him and took counsel with the young men who had grown up with him and stood before him" (v. 8). The young men told him to be harsh, and he foolishly did as they said.

This isn't to say our peers always give terrible counsel, but we shouldn't avoid counsel from older folks because we don't like it. We should hear their counsel and measure it by the ultimate source of wisdom, God's Word. That's why I'm encouraging you to specifically spend time with godly older people.

They may be out of touch, and they may still be using flip phones from the nineties, but that doesn't mean their counsel is worthless. Just don't ask them anything about technology. The amazing thing is, all of us are sinners, and we all struggle with the same things in different ways. While my older friends may not have the exact same issues as I do, they've likely had some of those same issues in different forms.

Matt and I work at the same church, and I'm always dropping into his office, even though I have to endure severe verbal abuse, in a godly way. One afternoon I was asking him about what he does when he's in a dry season spiritually.

For some reason, I was hoping for some magical answer, but he matter-of-factly said something to the effect of, "Keep reading your Bible until you feel like it." He'd struggled many times with the same thing I had, and he helped me see there's no magical thing I hadn't discovered yet. We're sinners, and

God draws us to Himself by His Word. I knew that, but I really needed to hear it that day. He'd already been there a million times before.

It's not just him, though. One of the reasons I'm so big on relationships with older Christians is because I've benefited from them in such a rich way. Every significant season of growth in my Christian life has been marked by relationships with older, more mature Christians. Sometimes they are twice my age like Matt, and other times they are five or ten years older than I am. They are truly gifts from God.

WHERE AM I SUPPOSED TO FIND THESE OLD PEOPLE?

I don't mean for you to start picking up random old people from nursing homes (though you should feel free to do that). I think the most natural thing to do is to get to know some of the older members in your church. Take them out to lunch and ask them how they came to know Christ. Ask them about God's grace in their lives. Get some counsel for the difficult things you're wrestling through.

If there are no older folks for you to go to, then just keep searching until you find one. I'm not saying that you're destined for spiritual immaturity until you become besties with someone who was born in the 1920s. I'm just saying, don't overlook such a sweet gift from the Lord.

Another natural way of gaining wisdom would be strengthening your relationship with your mom or dad, if they're believers. Relationships with family can be complicated, but you may be ignoring a well of grace God has provided for you. A few times in Proverbs we see encouragement to heed wisdom from parents. For example, Proverbs 13:1 says, "A wise son heeds his father's instruction, but a mocker does not respond to rebukes" (NIV). And Proverbs 1:8 says, "Listen, my son, to your father's instruction and do not forsake your mother's teaching" (NIV). This is a great way to obey Jesus by honoring your parents.

WHEN OLD PEOPLE ARE WRONG

As we've already said a few times, age does not always equal wisdom. So what happens when you get counsel from someone older that you think is wrong? First, you should check their counsel with God's. We should never, like Rehoboam, ignore counsel simply because we don't like it. Second, you should seek counsel from others to confirm that your understanding of God's Word is true. If it is, then without disrespecting the first counselors, you should obey God rather than man.

I remember that when I was about to go to college, I had some disagreements with my dad. My dad was loving and wise, but we didn't agree about what I should do after high school. He was very clear that he thought it was a bad idea for me to go to Bible college, and his reasons were logical, but still I disagreed. I thought it would be wise and God glorifying to get a biblical education. I got counsel from others as well, and I decided to go against my father's counsel. I took pains to make sure I did it in a respectful way, and eventually he came around and was happy for me.

I went through a similar situation when I got married. And again with leaders when I was moving from one church to another. There are times when godly people you respect will give you counsel you disagree with. We should always seek to be faithful to God and ask that He would give us wisdom. But we should tread carefully and not take going against counsel lightly.

FULL STEAM AHEAD

We should love age instead of despising it. John Mayer addresses our fear of age on his album *Continuum*, confessing to his father in a song that he is scared of growing old. His father then weighs in, saying, "I tried my hand / John, honestly we'll never stop this train."[1]

His dad's words in those lyrics are wise. I think he's basically saying that no matter what we do we can't stop time, so it's neither helpful nor effective to try. How should we view old age? We should neither fear it for ourselves, nor despise it in others.

Instead we should embrace what's good about it. We should receive wisdom from those who are older and seek to be those who give out wisdom when we get older. Age is certainly more than a number. It's a number that represents experience, and that's a well worth tapping into.

12

THE GREY RULE

When I first became a Christian, I had to rethink everything. How was I supposed to interact with my parents now? What about my friends? What about girls? Should I change the kind of music I write? I wanted Jesus to get glory from every nook and cranny of my life.

I took aim at the most visible targets first—like foul language and spiritual apathy. But I was also searching for less obvious areas of my life where Jesus wasn't getting the glory He deserved. I was poking all around my soul, peeking behind the refrigerator and lifting up the couch cushions. There was plenty of built-up filth to be dealt with. Some dirt was easy to turn from; other things were much harder.

At the time, music dominated my life. I had read far more lyrics in CD jackets than I had passages in Scripture. I was more familiar with my favorite rappers' rhyme schemes than parallelisms in the psalms. I remember sitting in my bedroom with my headphones blaring, dissecting Jay-Z's lyrics and trying to memorize my favorite Outkast songs. I had pictures of my favorite rappers cut out from *The Source* magazines and album covers printed from the Internet taped all over my wall. I was in love with music.

I turned my stereo on the moment I woke up, and I dozed off each night listening to something. I listened to my headphones on the thirty-five-minute drive to school, sneakily listened to music during study hall, and rapped with my friends during lunch. I listened to music while I did my homework, wrote music when I was done, and continued to listen while I brushed my teeth before bed. The only time I wasn't listening to music was at the dinner table with my family. Understandably, I couldn't overlook such an important area.

When I looked at my music with my new, redeemed eyes, I started to notice things I'd never seen before. Not everything was bad, but a lot of it was. Lyrics that used to make me smile made me scratch my head, and some of them actually made me angry. Rappers artfully tore down other men made in God's image and reduced wonderfully made women to 3-D posters, worth nothing more than lustful stares. R&B

singers detailed their sexual escapades and made lust seem honorable.

Something wasn't right. Music meant so much to me and brought me so much joy, but then I was torn. Surely God didn't approve of what some of those artists were saying, and I didn't want to displease Him. I didn't want the soundtrack of my life to be music that embraced and glorified the very things Jesus died to pay for. I had to do *something*. I shoved my cherished collection of hundreds of CDs under my bed and vowed to listen to all "Christian" music.

It wasn't easy. It was like telling old friends we couldn't chill like we used to. But I was willing to sacrifice the music I loved because I loved Jesus more. I went to the Christian bookstore and bought a ton of CDs, some traditional gospel and some hip-hop. Honestly, some of the stuff I bought was terrible. But I didn't realize it at the time because I was being encouraged by it. When you're starving, leftover Ramen noodles taste like steak. Some of it was amazing, though, and ended up being a huge part of why I started to write edifying music myself. God continued to make me more like Him during that season.

SINCERE BUT WRONG

As I look back, I'm grateful that I was willing to choose God over my music. I desperately needed to break away from the music I was listening to. I had been liberated from the prison of my sin, but the music I loved kept me close to the cell where

I'd been. I don't think I would have matured at that stage in my life had I not made some kind of significant change.

My zeal was praiseworthy, but my perspective was shallow. As far as Christians go, I was fresh out of the womb and still in diapers, but you couldn't tell that to my zeal. I was running full speed and didn't plan on hitting the brakes. And in the process, I made every issue black and white, cut and dry, straightforward.

Here's what I mean: as far as I was concerned, songs about Jesus were good, and songs about other things were bad. Even if those songs sounded good, we shouldn't be listening to them. Now, I wouldn't have said it that way, but that's certainly how I functioned.

I remember riding somewhere with my youth pastor, and as we talked, I was distracted for a moment by the music thumping in the background. At first I thought he had discovered some groundbreaking Christian R&B, and I wanted to check it out. But as I listened closer I realized it was just regular R&B. I was appalled! There was nothing foul or untrue about the songs, but they weren't about Jesus! I didn't say anything to him at the time, but I sat there and judged him in my heart until we reached our destination.

I thought my stance on music was the only stance you could hold, and I looked down on those who disagreed. I praise God today for my sincere intentions, but I wince at my immaturity. As time passed, I realized things are way more complex than I thought, and God has matured my perspective.

LEAVE ROOM FOR GREY

There are many moral issues that are black and white. Preaching the gospel is good, and punching little old ladies is bad. But there are many other areas that aren't so straight-forward. We sometimes call them grey areas. How do we make decisions in areas where there's no explicit biblical command? Paul didn't instruct the Corinthians about so-called secular music, so what do I do?

I want to tell you about a very simple rule I try to fol-low in these so-called grey areas. I call it "the grey rule." It's nothing monumental or even original. In fact, I first heard it years ago in a sermon, and I've heard a few people say similar things over the years. But just because something's simple doesn't mean it's not helpful.

Here's the grey rule: embrace things that lead you closer to Jesus, and reject things that lead you away from Jesus. Pretty simple, right? As an example, let's think about how it applies to media: music, TV, movies, video games, social media, magazines, etc.

MEDIA IS GOOD

I'll start by reminding you that media is good. It's not inher-ently bad or even neutral; it's good. It can be tempting to condemn media as a product of the evil one because of the ways it's often used, but we should be careful not to give the evil one too much credit. Paul warned Timothy about those who "forbid marriage and require abstinence from foods that God created to be received with thanksgiving by those who believe and know the truth. For everything created by God is good" (1 Tim. 4:3–4). It's not holy to call good things evil.

God created all things, including communication. He also created sound, vision, and beauty. Media is what happens when human beings, created in God's image, reshape and reimagine the beautiful gifts God has given us to make something new. When we communicate and create, we imitate our Creator and hold up a faint picture of Him for the world to see.

Rejecting media altogether is essentially turning up our noses when He offers us a merciful gift, and it robs Him of the glory He deserves. Media, in itself, is a good thing, and we should be careful about calling things evil when God has already called them good.

We confuse the issue when we attack good things instead of the real enemy—our own hearts. Hip-hop is not the problem, and neither is that new video-game console. Sin is the problem, and it always has been. Media is often foul, but not because media was created by Satan. It's because people are fallen, and this is what happens when you place good gifts into the hands of sinful people.

Imagine me letting my two-year-old son play with my iPhone. Say he accidentally calls 9-1-1 repeatedly for fifteen minutes straight. When the cops show up at my door, it would be foolish for me to exclaim, "That stupid iPhone!"

The problem wasn't the phone; it was the person holding it. The same principle applies with media. Let's make sure we point the blame in the right direction.

With that in mind, how can we enjoy the good gift of media without being corrupted by it in the process? Scripture doesn't give us a list of acceptable media, thus it's a grey area. That means we have to ask ourselves, how can we approach media consumption in a way that honors God? Grey doesn't mean "do what you want"; it means apply biblical principles to the situation. And with those biblical principles, we can think about what draws us to Jesus and what pushes us away.

FIVE PRINCIPLES

I'm not going to give you a list of what rating is permissible or which genres of music are acceptable, because that's neither helpful nor biblical. I'm going to give you five principles.

Be active, not passive

We shouldn't just let media wash over us; otherwise we may be swept away with the tide. We should engage with it. We should ask questions about it and engage with the content. As you enjoy it, treat it like a discussion. A book I read gave some helpful questions to ask:

1. What's the story?
2. Where am I (in the world of the text)?
3. What's good and true and beautiful about it?

4. What's false and ugly and perverse about it (and
   how do I subvert that)?

5. How does the gospel apply here?[1]

Media most definitely influences how we see the world
and awakens desires that lurk in our souls. We have to actively
engage with what we're taking in—even when we're taking in
"Christian" media. Sometimes movies claim to teach Christian
themes, but instead are nothing more than sanitized versions
of worldly messages. "Believe in yourself" and "Be a self-made
man" are not in the Bible. So engage with the content.

Know yourself

This will be scandalous for some and mundane for others,
but these days I do listen to some secular music, if by *secular*
you mean music that doesn't talk about Jesus. ("Secular" is
a strange and unhelpful category, but that's a discussion for
another book.) I feel no conviction when I listen to Stevie
Wonder, who's written some of the best love songs of all
time. I enjoy listening to rappers voice their worldviews while
I mentally engage with their arguments.

Additionally, I know what kind of music encourages me,
and I intentionally listen to that. Sometimes I want to hear
biblical truth, so I'll put on some doctrine-heavy hip-hop (or
watch some sermons). Other times I'll search the charts and
explore some new stuff I've never heard before.

No matter what I'm listening to, however, I proceed
with caution. I will not take in media that causes me to

stumble. That's transgressing the grey rule. I know myself well enough to know what I can and cannot listen to. For example, there's an album I love that has a couple of songs with detailed sexual content. I skip those songs because I know they're bad for my soul.

It's easy to convince myself something is harmless, but I have to remember that my soul is more important than my media intake. It's also good to talk over things with others who know you well. They can help you guard against self-deceit.

That brings me to the third principle.

Keep watch over your soul

Sin is nothing to play with, so if certain media causes you to sin, get away from it! Some of us need to get rid of some of our apps and erase some of our music. There is too much at stake! Our eternities are not worth entertainment or cultural awareness. There is no amount of connectivity or relevance that is worth the health of your soul.

Use media in moderation

We can't allow our every second to be dominated by media of different kinds. I've noticed that the first thing I do when I have a free second is check my phone. I could think or go over the scripture I've been memorizing, but instead I read a list about "Fifteen things that remind you of the nineties." Oversaturating ourselves with social media can lead to a lack of solitude and deep thought. It's good to unplug sometimes for the sake of your soul. This is part of thinking about what brings you closer to Jesus.

Receive media with thanksgiving

In every expression of creativity, there is a faint picture of our Creator on display. As those who know this God, we recognize Him when we see Him. We can praise God for His creativity and thank Him for His mercy in sharing it with us.

If we simply retreat from everything instead of taking the time to navigate it, we'll be missing out on beautiful gifts from our Lord. Not only that, but pop culture can be a huge factor in our engagement with others. After all, media is both an influencer and a mirror; it affects attitudes and reflects them. Again, we should proceed with caution, but we should partake and enjoy to the glory of God.

This is one of the main ways we glorify God with our media intake. We enjoy it and worship God as the originator of it.

LOOKING BACK

Teenage me would probably rebuke present-day me. I would probably call present-day me worldly and compromising, but that's my past immaturity speaking. Don't be like I was. Accept the grey. And when others disagree with you or decide to partake where you abstain, don't condemn them. Share concerns where you have them and be gracious with them. God has been more than gracious with us.

The Bible has given us more than enough principles to work with. Grey areas don't mean free-for-all; they mean navigating a more complex road. The mature Christian doesn't just ask, "What can I do?" but "What can I do to glorify God?" even when it's not so black and white.

13

RUDE AWAKENING

In the summer of 2007, I was at a turning point in my life and feeling good. I had one year of college under my belt, and my grades had been pretty good. I went on my first real nationwide tour, and I was feeling inspired heading into my second album. I was also preparing to talk to my future father-in-law, to tell him I was interested in his daughter and wanted to pursue her with the hopes of marriage. It was a good season of life.

When I arrived back on campus after my summer break,

I expected to have another year like the last. I was excited about my classes and praying that God would help me take advantage of the biblical education available to me. I assumed everything would go according to plan; I didn't think I'd encounter anything out of the ordinary.

As my classes started, I was ready to get back into the swing of things. One evening, while eating some strange cafeteria mixture with friends, I noticed I was more tired than usual. I slapped hands with my friends, excused myself from the table, and strolled down the hill toward my dorm, making plans for how I would get my work done for the next day. I walked into my building, stumbled down the hallway, and plopped down on the bed like a crash dummy.

When I finally came out of my sleep coma, I realized I hadn't woken to the sound of my alarm. I poked my head out from under my bunk and looked up to realize my roommate had already left for the day. That wasn't a good sign. I looked at my phone and saw I had missed a few calls, as well as most of my classes for the day. I hadn't planned on using up my absences so early in the semester, but I couldn't do anything about it at that point, so I took a drive down the street to grab some food.

I expected to catch up on my missed work and resume life as normal, but that wasn't what happened. Instead, I was still exhausted, and a depressing cycle began. I would be extremely tired in the evening, fall asleep early, wake up late, nap most of the day, and be tired in the evening all over again. I was sleeping about eighteen hours a day and stumbling around like a zombie for the other six.

It was clear something was wrong, so I went to the doctor's office. To make a long story short, he misdiagnosed me with a virus, and then, when I didn't get any better, he said the virus had given me chronic fatigue syndrome. He said I should just wait it out. *Wait it out?* I hadn't gotten anything done for weeks, I was failing all my classes, and I felt terrible.

When I didn't get any better, I decided to move on and see an infectious disease specialist. He did a million tests to see if there was a simpler explanation, but there wasn't one. He, too, diagnosed me with chronic fatigue syndrome. He said a virus doesn't cause it, but that doctors weren't sure what actually causes it. He was more helpful than the previous doctor, but still there was nothing he could do except check in on me and tell me to eat healthy.

That was a difficult year for me. I failed virtually all my classes during the next twelve months. I was trying to keep up with my school load, but my body kept running out of gas and my teachers kept running out of grace. I pretty much disappeared for a year and spent most of my time in my room. While I would eventually get a little better, my life has never been the same since. Life struck me and left its mark, like a dark bruise from a punch. But the black eye that sometimes hovers over my soul has taught me valuable lessons that the sunny days never could.

I am not invincible. On the contrary, it seems that I'm extremely vincible. And the Lord decided to use a trial to make that clear to me. I never actually thought I was untouchable, but at the same time I assumed my life would continue to be carefree. This was no doubt youthful ignorance on my part. I saw my health as a given instead of a gift, and I never imagined some of it would be taken away so soon.

Energy was something I just always had. Sure, I would get tired sometimes, but when I woke up in the morning, my energy level would always be there to greet me along with the sunshine. I never really thought about energy until I didn't have any; I never thought about how vital it is. Energy is the gasoline that fuels our every action, thought, and feeling. It powers every minute of our lives, like the battery in your smartphone. If it doesn't get recharged, all your fancy apps and features don't run. For some reason my body had stopped recharging.

I recognize my trial is minuscule compared to many, even most, in our fallen world. But that doesn't make it any easier. While I used to feel free to run from one stage of life to the next, I was now feeling held back. All of a sudden it felt like there was a dark cloud over my mind and an anchor tied to my soul, pulling me down with ill intent. It sounds dramatic, I know, but it's how I felt. My energy was gone, and all that remained was a feeling of emptiness. I wasn't ready for my energy to be taken, but God was ready to take it.

There are mercies from God that we are too confident will always remain. Often we think new mercies are automatic and should be expected, like the click we hear when we lock our car doors. God's mercies are indeed new each morning, but we shouldn't assume He'll grant us the same ones He gave us yesterday. Every single breath, every solitary heartbeat, every ounce of energy is its own individual gift from God. And while He delights to give us those gifts, He's never obligated to continue.

Why have I taken so much time to tell you about how I felt? Because I want you to be grateful for the numerous kindnesses the Lord has thrown your way. But I also want to remind you that you aren't invincible either.

DEATH IS COMING

I teach a weekly Bible study at a local high school, and one of the reasons I love the students is because they always react so honestly. In one of the first Bible studies I led there, we looked at Job 14:1–2: "Man who is born of a woman is few of days and full of trouble. He comes out like a flower and withers; he flees like a shadow and continues not." After reading the passage, I asked the students, "What do you think Job means with all this language about few days, withering, and continuing not?"

They were quiet, either because they weren't sure or they didn't want to speak up. So I answered my own question: "Job is saying all of us have troubled lives and all of us will die."

I must have said it matter-of-factly, because one girl got a concerned, confused look on her face and said, "Why do you say it like that?" I wasn't disappointed that she was shocked, because I wanted that truth to shock them. While many of those students' lives are far from perfect, being young has a way of blinding us to the whole truth.

When we live assuming that everything will be swell, or at least continue as is, we ignore the truth Job points to in this scripture. In his lament about his own suffering, Job testifies to the truth about all of us. We won't always be here, and even while we are, our lives will be full of difficulties.

Our world is messed up. And even though death is wrong, it's real. It's not how it's supposed to be, but it's how it is for now. One day Jesus will kill death for good, but until then death is a reality for every single one of us. And before death even gets to us, a million smaller wrongs will have already encountered us.

Our bodies are messed up, our families are messed up, and our minds are messed up. The older we get, the more this will become painfully clear.

The question is not whether or not you will face trials. The question is, how will you respond when you do?

RESPONDING TO TRIALS

When you're going through a really hard time, some people don't know what to say. As a result, they often throw out meaningless clichés or trite attempts to cheer you up. I've always had a problem with cliché phrases that don't mean anything to the person saying them and don't actually help the person hearing them. Silly things like "Chin up" and "It'll get better." Really? How do you know? You don't do anybody any favors by giving them light and fluffy hopes that aren't rooted in anything. When deep pain hits, we need rock-solid truth to sustain us.

During his bout with cancer, the atheist writer Christopher Hitchens voiced similar frustration with some of the meaningless phrases that get thrown around. He spent a few pages attacking one of them in his book *Mortality*. He said, "In particular, I have slightly stopped issuing the announcement that 'whatever doesn't kill me makes me stronger.'" He went on to say, "In the brute physical world . . . there are all too many things that could kill you, don't kill you, and then leave you considerably weaker."[1] Can't you just feel the joy?

It sounds depressing, but I think Hitchens is right in a sense. It is quite possible that we can go through difficult things that only weaken us and bring us closer to death. Even the most positive people can be broken down by the brutality of our fallen world. Optimism can only survive so many beatings until it breaks and reality finally chokes it out. Phrases that once sounded cute now seem worthless. But at the same time, is it possible the well-meaning sentiment Hitchens attacked is ever true? I think so.

WHEN IS IT TRUE?

"What doesn't kill me makes me stronger" can be true, but only if there's something beyond this life. If this life, this world, and this body are all there is, Hitchens is right. That statement is a lie. It would be like saying, "What doesn't total my car makes it stronger." That's ridiculous. You'd have to ignore the truth to believe that. But if our temporary trials have some kind of eternal meaning, that changes everything.

Paul wrote, "And we know that in all things God works for the good of those who love him, who have been called according to his purpose" (Rom. 8:28 NIV). This verse is sometimes abused, but it's one of the most beautiful promises in all Scripture. This doesn't mean Christians are invincible. All of us will face trials, but we can't finally be defeated by them. Even our worst enemies, like suffering and death, become our friends in Christ because they ultimately work in our favor.

It's like the black watch I'm wearing on my wrist right now. It's waterproof. That doesn't mean that when I wash the dishes or go outside in a storm it won't get wet. Waterproof means even though it gets wet, it can't be destroyed. For the Christian, all things working for our good doesn't mean storms can't touch us; it means they can't destroy us. Instead, God turns everything that happens to us and uses it in our ultimate favor.

How exactly can these devastating trials make us stronger? Here are three ways (with significant overlap):

Trials can make us depend on Jesus

When I feel like everything in my life is going well, my heart immediately retreats into self-dependence. It never fails. I start to pray less because I subconsciously assume I don't lack anything. I become proud because I think I'm the reason everything's going well. In those times, I forget that God is the giver of good gifts and I still need Him to sustain me. I assume I'm entitled to all His mercies.

But when trials come our way, they show us our own weakness. Sickness reminds us how fragile we are, layoffs remind us that hard work doesn't guarantee anything, and conflict reminds us that we need Jesus in every area of our lives.

Second Corinthians 12 is a comfort to me in times of weakness. Paul recognized that God gave him a trial to "keep [him] from becoming conceited" (v. 7 NIV). And Paul said he boasted gladly in his weakness and that he was content with all kinds of trials (vv. 9–10). How could Paul be content and even glad about his trials? I think Paul was saying that the trials made clear he needed God's grace and power. Self-dependence is weakness, and dependence on Christ is strength. Paul said, "When I am weak, then I am strong" (v. 10 NIV).

Trials can make us more like Jesus

We'll never be able to endure devastating trials until we realize that our comfort and good health isn't what's most important. Comfort and health are good things that God delights to give us. But God's primary will for our lives is that we would be like Jesus. And He's even willing to use trials to accomplish that will. "[God] disciplines us for our good, that we may share his holiness" (Heb. 12:10). Training in God's gym may hurt sometimes, but He will make us stronger.

James 1:2 comes to mind, where he tells us to "count it all joy, my brothers, when you meet trials of various kinds." The reason we should count it as joy is the Christlike character it produces. Our humility is more important than our happiness. It's better to be physically weak and spiritually strong.

Trials can make us long to be with Jesus

Our hearts are weakened by sin, and we often find ourselves longing for more of what this world has to offer. But when the temporary joys of this world are taken from us, we're reminded that earth is not our home. Our citizenship is elsewhere.

I love staying in nice hotels, and when I do, I try to take advantage of all the perks. But then I start to miss my wife, and then I realize I don't have the clothes I meant to bring, and then I realize room service is about half as good as my wife's cooking. All that reminds me this hotel isn't my home. Unmet desires make me long to be at home. This earth isn't where we belong, and trials remind us that our paradise is elsewhere, with our Lord. There will be no unmet desires in heaven because our Lord will satisfy all our longings. He'll abolish pain and pour His grace out on us forever.

The next time you have friends going through tough times, remind them that even the most tragic circumstances can make us stronger. Not through positive thinking and optimism, but through real hope and real change. And when you're going through a difficult season, let it draw you closer to Christ. Don't be afraid; the Lord is with you. The believer's hope is beyond the grave, so even what kills us can make us stronger.

UPDATE

As I write this chapter, I still haven't been healed. It continues to complicate every area of my life. In fact, the book is
being turned in a week late because chronic fatigue left me
bedridden for a few days the week it was due. I'm still praying
the Lord will heal me, and that He'll give me grace to glorify Him in my weakness. My energy is never the same from
week to week, but my God is. I look forward to the day when
I'll be resurrected with a brand-new body that's flawless. But
until then I glory in the God who never gets tired and never
deteriorates.

> *Even youths shall faint and be weary,*
>   *and young men shall fall exhausted;*
> *but they who wait for the LORD shall renew their strength;*
>   *they shall mount up with wings like eagles;*
> *they shall run and not be weary;*
>   *they shall walk and not faint.*
>
>   (ISA. 40:30–31)

• Part Three •

POINTING UP

14

ARE YOU ONE OF
THOSE CHRISTIANS?

When I tell someone I'm a Christian, I never know what kind of response to expect. When I'm in some places, like my hometown, Dallas, that's no more surprising than saying I have ten fingers. Not only do we in Dallas have Christian people, but we also have Christian T-shirts and license plates. We even have our own churchy language (it's kind of like pig Latin, but more sanctified, and should only be used in church or around churchy people). But when I'm outside the Bible Belt, it's not assumed that everything breathing has submitted to Jesus.

You should see the looks on people's faces when I pull out my Bible during flights. I interpret their raised left eyebrows to mean, "Really? This guy? I never would've guessed it." It's possible they all have some kind of weird eyebrow twitch, but I doubt it. I don't know if it's my age, if it's how I dress, or if I just have an agnostic vibe to me, but people seem to be shocked.

One guy, whom I sat next to on a large jet, actually said it out loud. He looked at me and confessed, "Y'know, when you got on this plane, I had already prejudged you. I'll admit it; my brain basically exploded when you pulled out your Bible." I knew it! As soon as I saw him, I pinned him as the type of guy who judges others as soon as he sees them.

Sometimes people's responses depend on what kind of Christian they perceive me to be. Maybe they'll ask a few probing questions to figure out if I am just a Christian or if I am "one of *those* Christians." You know, the ones everybody loves to dislike; the kind who get all their values from a really old book and insist that God wrote it so it must be true; the kind who defend "traditional" marriage on CNN and refuse to change their minds. Brothers and sisters, a reputation precedes us.

OUR REPUTATION

Recently I read a satirical essay by a popular author who gave an outlandish picture of a devout Christian. He seemed to be writing in character, so I don't want to assume this is what he thinks about all serious followers of Christ, but he did capture the worldview of many.

He began the essay like this:

> If I ruled the world, the first thing I'd do is concede all power to the *real* King who, in case you don't happen to know, is named Jesus Christ. A lot of people have managed to forget this lately so the second thing I'll do is remind them of it. Not only would I bring back mandatory prayer in school, but I'd also institute it at work. Then skating rinks and airports. Wherever people live or do business, they shall know His name. Christ's picture will go on all our money, and if you had your checks specially printed with sailboats or shamrocks on them, too bad for you because from here on out, the only images allowed will be of Him, or maybe of me reminding you of how important He is.[1]

You have to admit that paragraph is kind of funny. What's not so funny is that this is how many people think of Christians—backwoodsy, mean-spirited, and irrational. They think we're unintelligent, outdated, and stubborn. Not only that, but they think we're judgmental and self-righteous. When they think *Christian*, they think of people with their noses in the air and their fingers pointed at others. And they see that even the most stuck-up religious people have issues, but they're refusing to admit it.

Who wants to be that guy? And who wants to follow a Savior who turns people into someone like that? No one does. But no one has to. The world despises hypocrisy, and so does Jesus. Let's rise above that. Let's be sin-admitting, Christ-trusting, people-loving believers. Let's show the world another picture of what it means to follow Christ. Let's love people even when they don't love us.

ANOTHER PICTURE

The turning point for a lot of people is when they interact with a Christian who is different from what they thought Christians were like. One of my good friends thought being saved meant being an old lady with peppermints in her purse. Then he started attending a campus ministry's Bible study and went to a Christian conference in Atlanta.

He saw people who looked like him on the outside, but they seemed to have different goals and desires than he did. They had *J*s on their feet, but they didn't use them to run to wickedness. Their clothes were even baggy like his (this was the early 2000s, a rough time for hip-hop fashion). He didn't have a category for Christians who looked and acted like that. And then a man took the stage and preached a message about the perfect God-man who sacrificed Himself to purchase imperfect sinners with His own blood. My friend would never be the same.

I know a lot of people who think they're rejecting Jesus Christ, but what they're actually rejecting is a man who doesn't exist. They're rejecting the Jesus they heard about, but not the Jesus of the Scriptures. A Christian's job is to live in such a way that shows off the real Jesus, the all-powerful, almighty, sinner-loving King of the universe.

The sad truth is that some people will see genuine Christians and hear the true gospel preached, but they will still reject the Christ of that gospel. Most of us reading this book rejected the gospel when we first heard it. So although there are false things believed about Christianity that people hate, there are also true things about Christianity that people don't like.

WE'RE UNPOPULAR

I recognize that I've come of age during a very interesting time, where values that were once assumed are now despised. Though I think it would be inaccurate to refer to the America of the past as a "Christian" country, it's never been as anti-Christian as it is now. This isn't to say that there are no Christians in the United States or that religious freedom has altogether disappeared. But there's no doubt that things are changing and deeply held Christian beliefs are not to be celebrated. And if it's up to some, they're not even to be tolerated.

I don't mean to sound like a conspiracy-theorizing doomsday prophet with canned food stacked ceiling high in my basement. I assure you I only keep enough canned food in the house for the week ahead of me. But we do need to think about what it means to be faithful to Christ in a culture where our presence is less and less appreciated.

Stop acting so surprised

Where in Scripture did Jesus say, "You will follow Me, and everyone will love you for it"? To save you the time searching for it, I'll answer that for you: nowhere. Instead, He said things like, "You will be hated by all for my name's sake" (Matt. 10:22).

Jesus offended people when He came, and He still offends people now. His first followers were persecuted, as His followers have been all throughout history, and we shouldn't expect to be the exception. Christianity was never meant to be popular. If you don't believe me, take a look around the globe. Our brothers and sisters are being slaughtered—specifically for their faith—every single day.

Why do people persecute us? One of the reasons is because they love the dark rather than the light. In fact, Jesus tells us all of us do. We're like the walking dead in zombie movies, who stay in the dark because the light physically pains them. All of us are born allergic to the light, so we shouldn't be surprised when the light angers people. We are dark-dwellers and will be until Christ shines light in our hearts.

If you're a Christian reading this and thinking, *What's he talking about? Everyone loves everything I say*, you should ask yourself whether what you're saying is true.

Fall out of love with being cool

Some of the people reading this aren't cool in the first place, so maybe this doesn't apply to you. But if you are still holding on to that, I encourage you to let it go. We cannot lay our lives down for such a divisive Man while at the same time being liked by everyone. You can still dress like a rapper or a hipster, but just be aware that other rappers and hipsters might not appreciate your presence. Cool is fickle, and we can't live for it.

Be compassionate instead of being combative

Love people, don't fight them. That essayist I quoted earlier didn't completely fabricate that picture of Christians. He produced a portrait of a real minority among those who claim Christ. I've seen people who think the way to follow Jesus is through scathing Facebook posts, hateful picket signs, and deceitful schemes. Their zeal has been terribly misplaced.

Our battle is not against those who hate us, but against the demonic thoughts that hold them captive. They've been deceived! We fight not against flesh and blood, but against spiritual evil (Eph. 6:12). Which brings me to the next point.

Tell others about Christ

Second Corinthians 10 talks about our spiritual fight and doesn't mention weapons or picket signs. Instead, it refers to a message, the gospel. And only the gospel has divine power to destroy the strongholds in our culture.

This doesn't mean you should never have a conversation about anything other than Jesus. "So Tasha, how's your day been?"

"Fine. But speaking of days, are you ready for the dreadful day of the Lord?"

Take it easy. Remember that love part. Get to know people. You'll like them more than you think, and then your service to them will come from love and not some desire to win or accomplish something. People are not projects but precious creatures made in the image of God.

Stand firm

All of us feel the temptation to buckle under the pressure. Most of us are grieved for those who've been offended by others who claim Christ. We don't understand everything in the Bible, and we can't defend every verse that we've never studied before. But we should continue to study Scripture and stand firm on God's Word.

Realize the world wants to proselytize and convert you. They want you to abandon the Lord and admit you've been wrong. They want you to concede that Christianity is opposed to science, morals, and progress in our society. And sometimes they may sound convincing to you. My encouragement is to stand firm. There is nothing more certain than our God and what He's done for us in Christ. Don't let anything convince you otherwise.

People will call you intolerant and bigoted. But stand firm. Contrary to what our culture teaches us, there are worse things than offending other people. One of them is giving people a false picture of who God is. Another is condoning things that will lead to their destruction.

Honestly repent of your shortcomings

One of the things that turns others off is the hypocrisy and self-righteousness they see so often. But when we're honest about our shortcomings and repent of our sins, we get to show our hope to others. Don't miss gospel opportunities by pretending to be perfect.

Pray

There is nothing more loving you can do for people than talk to God about them. I've also found that when I pray for people regularly, God grows my love for them.

As the days go on, we don't know how people will respond when we tell them we're Christians or when we pull our Bibles out on flights. We don't know how people will perceive Christians in ten years. But what we do know is our God will remain faithful. And we should pray that He allows us to be faithful to Him.

15

EVERYTHING IS SACRED

Have you ever heard kids ask questions? They have an amazing curiosity that seems to have no end. That magical question "why?" can go on for hours and hours. One comedian joked that by the time these conversations end, they can be so abstract that you don't even know who you are anymore. Well, it seems there's a little child in my soul that likes to ask why, but it's not about abstract ideas; it's about everyday things.

I'm not very easily motivated. The fact that something

needs to be done doesn't seem to be enough. I need extra motivation, which is why the little child in me asks, "Why?" There are some people who are naturally driven, and the fact that something needs to get done is enough motivation for them. My wife is one of those people; I am not.

In order for me to get anything done, I need to sense that I'm doing something grand. I'm a big-picture guy, and I'm rarely drawn to details or tedious tasks. Unfortunately, details and tedious tasks are the majority of real life. This is probably why I struggled so much in high school, even after I became a Christian. My math classes seemed useless and homework felt like a waste of my time.

I know I'm not the only one who finds it difficult to be motivated. We all have those weeks where it feels like a never-ending cycle of blah. Even as I write these words, I'm struggling to keep pushing with this book.

Young Christians like you and me are often zealous but irresponsible. We want to be used by God, but all the little things—like clocking in at our desk jobs—seem like obstacles to that desire. Of course we have to work if we want to eat, but it would be great if we could use our time helping needy people or sharing the gospel instead.

One of the reasons we struggle is because we forget that Jesus is the Lord of all. When I say Lord of all, I don't just mean Lord of all people; I mean Lord of all things and spheres of life. It's easy for us to section off our lives into little quadrants. There's the fun stuff, the family stuff, the boring stuff, and the spiritual stuff. But the Bible doesn't recognize any area of our lives that's not spiritual. God made every sphere of life, He rules over every sphere of life, and He can be glorified in every sphere of life. This means *everything* is sacred.

Some of you are familiar with Paul's words to the Corinthians: "Whether you eat or drink or whatever you do, do it all for the glory of God" (1 Cor. 10:31 NIV). In the passage, he was talking to the church about how their actions affected one another. It's not enough to just think about yourself; you also have to think about the big picture—even when you're doing something as ordinary as eating a meal. God's great story is told in every nook and cranny of our lives, so nothing should be discarded as unimportant.

If you want to do big things for God, you shouldn't look elsewhere; you should start right where you are.

TRUE GREATNESS

When I'm working on something new, whether it's an album, a book, or a blog post, I find it helpful to watch other people be great. I love seeing their discipline and attention to detail. As I began working on this book, I started looking for interviews with authors of books that I'd enjoyed. I thought maybe I'd hear something that would inspire me or help me in my writing rhythm. Some were Christian authors or musicians like myself; others were fiction writers and atheists. I can learn from anyone who bears the image of God, which includes every human.

Alan Moore is the author of several graphic novels,

including the much-celebrated *Watchmen*. I was skeptical of graphic novels, but as I read *Watchmen* I loved the twists and plots of the story, and my mind was engaged as I interacted with the values of the characters in the world he created. I looked him up to see what he was like.

In a YouTube interview, a young woman asked Moore what advice he would give to young writers. He said, "If you're going to take on any artistic endeavor, treat writing as if it was a god. Treat writing as if it was some supernatural deity that you had to appease, that you had to do your very best work for, that nothing other than your best would be good enough. Treat it like that. Treat it that seriously. This is not just a career."[1]

There's something I really love about how seriously he takes his craft, but it's clear how different our worldviews are. I'm an ambitious artist, and I've sought to attempt things that people told me weren't possible. I obsess over my art and try to surround myself with great artists who will make me better. I honestly want to be great at what I do.

But while Moore and I share a love of art and an ambition for greatness, our motivations are very different. I don't think I have to imagine that my art is a god in order for me to take it seriously. I believe there is a very real God, who's very interested in the work I do, and He's interested in your work as well. We don't have to drum up any kind of phony motivation in order to feel like we're doing something grand, because when we do it for God, we *are* doing something grand.

BE FAITHFUL WHERE YOU ARE

Scripture doesn't try to get all of us to do one special thing in order to glorify God. Instead, it addresses all of us exactly where we are and tells us how God can be glorified right there. You can see this clearest in some of Paul's epistles in which he talked to husbands, wives, children, and even slaves. He didn't address whether or not their current situations were ideal, but instead he told them how they could glorify God while they were in them.

Ultimately, whatever it is you're doing, it's for God. Paul wrote to the Colossians: "Whatever you do, work heartily, as for the Lord and not for men, knowing that from the Lord you will receive the inheritance as your reward. You are serving the Lord Christ" (Col. 3:23–24). No matter where you are or what you're doing, your supervisor is Jesus. He's the one who will reward you, and He's the one you'll ultimately answer to.

Zeal is fantastic, but we have to get beyond the naive zeal that only gets excited about the "big stuff," like our next mission trip or next stage of life. Instead, we should be thinking most about how to be faithful in the everyday normal stuff. Because the normal is, well, normal.

POINT UP

What we do with our lives every day, whether at school, a desk job, or keeping the home in order, is our most basic opportunity to glorify God. That's what your role in His story looks like day in and day out. Instead of waiting to be offered a new role, play the current one well.

What picture of God are you showing to your coworkers? What about your classmates or the relatives you live with? Are you telling the right story?

One of the most interesting biographies I've read in a while is Walter Isaacson's biography of Steve Jobs. He was a genius who was passionate about everything. He obsessed over every detail and was deeply driven, almost in a worshipful way. That worship-like obsession led him to change the world. Unfortunately, he seemed to be worshipping something less than worthy.

As worshippers of the true God, what kind of passion does our worship fuel? What kinds of change will we make around us? The truth is, not much will change if we put God in the Sunday box and pretend like He has no interest in our daily lives. The question isn't whether or not He cares about your day-to-day life; it's whether or not you're going to offer it up to Him. Because everything you do is sacred.

16

A DISEASE WORTH SPREADING

When I was a kid, I used to pray for sickness. I wasn't praying for anything serious, just something like a cold. I wanted God to give me something that was mild enough that I didn't notice, but that was bad enough for my mom to notice and agree to let me stay home from school. And I'm not going to lie—I faked it a few times. I didn't like school, so sickness seemed far better. No class, plus staying at home all day on the couch in front of the TV? It was like a little dose of summer in the middle of the school year.

My mom probably knew I was faking it sometimes, but she couldn't just ignore it. Because if I actually was sick, she would feel bad for not believing me. The other reason she couldn't just ignore it was if I was contagious, I could infect other kids. It wasn't worth me making other kids sick.

What do you do if you see people sneeze or cough and then they reach their hands out to shake yours? You step away and back off. Why? Because you don't want to get what they have. Sickness can be contagious. Some kinds of sickness, like the common cold, are relatively harmless. But other kinds of sickness are a lot more serious, and I wouldn't dare laugh or make light of them. But what if there were a contagious disease worth spreading?

Forgive me for comparing glorious things to undesirable things, but I think it'll help us grasp the point. God's love and compassion are like a contagious illness; if you've truly been exposed to it, you can't help but pass it on to others. I don't mean in a pay-it-forward kind of way. I don't mean that if someone does something nice for you, you're now obligated to do something nice for someone else. Of course there's nothing wrong with that, but God doesn't have to be in your life for you to do that.

I'm talking about something that goes much deeper than obligation or duty. I'm talking about the kind of disease that gets into your soul and affects you. God's compassion is not a mere example for us to follow; it's the very thing He uses to make us want to follow Him. If you've received Christ, you've been exposed to the compassion of our God, and you should be looking to pass it on to others.

OUR WORLD IS MESSED UP

Have you looked around our world lately? It's a mess. Sometimes I'll talk to people who will ask me why God created such a messed-up world. Well, it's clear from Scripture that God didn't make the world this way; sin did. Adam and Eve's disobedience is commonly referred to as "the fall" (Gen. 3).

That horrific fall didn't just affect our relationship with God; it affected our relationship with everything. We're not fallen men and women living in a perfect world; all creation is fallen—for now. For example, work is a good thing that God created for us to take part in, but now work is difficult and toilsome. Animals that were under our rule are now prone to attack us, not to say anything of the conflicts we have with one another. Even the weather is against us, as we've seen with tornados, hurricanes, and tsunamis. Our world is a mess. It's almost like we've made creation angry, and it's swinging at us constantly, some of us taking more blows than others.

People are hurting. Many people don't have access to the most basic human needs, like water. Others are hurting and suffering at the hands of other human beings, who themselves are hurting. Everywhere we look we see the marks of the fall in the lives of our fellow human beings.

I wonder if that means anything to you. What comes to mind when you're at a stop sign waiting for an older man to cross the street, slowly moving his slumped and worn-down body to the other side? What do you think when you sit down by a young woman on the subway, bobbing her head and blocking out the world with her headphones? Better yet, what about when you pass the homeless man begging for money—what goes through your mind?

Many are tempted to look down on them and dismissively reject their pleas for help, maybe even urging them to get a job and take care of themselves. To most of us that seems obviously cruel and immoral. So we aren't rude at all, but we walk by without giving these persons a second thought.

He's just another man sitting on the corner. And after all, you're not treating him any differently than anybody else. You just want to take care of your business. We're sometimes completely oblivious to one another (especially now that we're so sucked into our phones).

This is particularly true in big cities where people are everywhere. Whenever there's a lot of something, we tend to forget its value. When there are millions of people bumping into one another at every twist and turn, we tend to see people as objects or props. They are no more significant to us than the traffic light or the seat we're in. But we couldn't be more wrong. There's not an insignificant person on this earth. All people are valuable creatures made in the image of the almighty God.

THE VALUE OF MAN

When I was in high school, I went to Italy on a class trip. I didn't appreciate the opportunity at the time, which is clear from the many times I got in trouble with my friends. We went into the Sistine Chapel and looked up at the ceiling where Michelangelo's famous painting is. The folks around me were in awe, pointing up and serenely taking in its beauty. My friends and I glanced up, decided it looked just like the pictures in our textbooks, and continued to make jokes with one another.

We were bored with it. We'd seen so much history and cool stuff that we didn't fully appreciate what we were looking at. We disrespected it and treated it like we were looking at a wall a kid colored with some crayons.

I was overlooking what made that painting precious: its beauty, its historical significance, who painted it, and what the painting portrayed. Its beauty is undeniable, it's one of the most famous paintings in history, Michelangelo is arguably the greatest painter in history, and he was attempting to represent the most important things of God.

Human beings are similarly valuable for those same four reasons.

- Our beauty: we are fearfully and wonderfully made.
- Our significance: we all play a very real role in God's story.

- Who created us: that homeless man is the craftsmanship of the God of the universe, a far greater artist than Michelangelo.
- What we were created to portray: we were created to show off God.

Because of the fall, we're distorted pictures of Him, but we're pictures nonetheless. Our world is the most valuable art gallery in existence, but we're so used to it we don't appreciate it.

Were someone to destroy the Sistine Chapel, those who understand its value would grieve. Likewise, when human beings suffer, we should be grieved. And our response should be not indifferent coldness but indiscriminate compassion.

Our goal should be to see people the way God sees them and to interact with them the way God would—in a loving and compassionate manner. But how can we know how God would treat people? Well, we can look at that one time when God came to earth and lived among us.

JESUS' COMPASSION

Our Lord Jesus was an incredible picture of compassion. Whenever I read the Gospels, I'm blown away at how many people Jesus mercifully healed, taught, and fed. Matthew noted that at one point "they brought him all the sick, those afflicted with various diseases and pains, those oppressed by demons, epileptics, and paralytics, and he healed them"

(Matt. 4:24). You'll notice that Jesus never did those things in exchange for any payment of any kind. He saw those He had created, and He decided to have mercy on them.

It's clear in the Gospels that the main purpose of Jesus' works was to point to Himself. Yet it's also clear that He was motivated by compassion for His image bearers: "When he saw the crowds, he had compassion on them" (Matt. 9:36 NIV); "He had compassion on them and healed their sick" (Matt. 14:14 NIV); "I have compassion on the crowd because they . . . have nothing to eat" (Matt. 15:32).

Of course the compassion of Jesus went much further than meeting physical needs. Jesus' merciful compassion would eventually lead Him to die on the cross for sinners. He saw that sinners were in need of a Savior, and He willingly laid down His life to meet their eternal need. Christians are those who have been made aware of that need and have put their faith in Jesus to meet it. We are those who have had a face-to-face encounter with the compassion of our God, and He's infected us with it.

WHAT PROVOKES OUR COMPASSION?

Scripture is clear that God didn't save us because we were good; God saved us because He is good. In Paul's letter to Titus, he went through a list of our sin problems and then said, "But when the goodness and loving kindness of God our Savior appeared, he saved us, not because of works done by us in righteousness, but according to his own mercy"

(Titus 3:4–5). God was motivated by mercy to save us. And that mercy should be seen in us as well.

It's clear that God expects such compassion from His people. Often in the Old Testament, God rebuked His people for their failure to obey Him. And as He laid out His case against them, He often pointed to their lack of compassion as evidence they hadn't trusted in Him. One example is in Isaiah 1:17, where He detailed for them what repentance looks like: "Learn to do good; seek justice, correct oppression; bring justice to the fatherless, plead the widow's cause."

When you put your faith in our compassionate God, it leads to a compassionate life. Paul talked to the Colossians about putting off their old ways and putting on their new ways. He said, "Put on then, as God's chosen ones, holy and beloved, compassionate hearts, kindness, humility, meekness, and patience" (Col. 3:12). Along with patience and humility, Paul encouraged them to put on compassion. These are all characteristics of the God who saved them, and all were displayed when Jesus served us with His death on the cross.

WITNESS OF COMPASSION

What does it say to the world when we claim to serve such a compassionate God, yet we look nothing like Him? I've seen many times where people's hearts are more open to the gospel when they see that someone really cares about them. Sometimes the best way to inform people about the love of Christ is by showing it to them in tangible ways.

Whenever I pass people who are asking for money on the street, I usually prefer to buy them meals. I never know their situations, but I know food is always helpful. If they'll accept it, I'll give it to them and pray for them. And I'm satisfied if that's the end of the interaction. But if they'll listen, I'll always tell them why I was led to help them out. Because God found me needy, and He graciously met my needs. I couldn't pay for my sin, but He sent Christ to pay for it. That's compassion at its greatest.

Showing compassion is one of the clearest ways we can visibly show people what the gospel looks like. Nothing can replace the proclamation of the good news, but good deeds often serve to buy time and someone's ear to hear it.

WHAT DO YOU DO?

Compassion shouldn't end with a tug on your heart. It should lead to loving acts. It should lead to good deeds. We don't praise Christ just for noticing our needs, but we also praise Him for meeting our needs. In similar fashion, we should be looking for ways to meet the needs of others.

But sometimes it's hard to know where to start. Not all of us are aware of great needs within our communities. Here's what I suggest.

Pay Attention
Often we miss the beautiful image bearers who are all around us. Our hearts are so filled with self that there's no

room left for compassion. The eyes of our hearts never get a chance to look out upon the world because they're too captivated by what they see in the mirror. It's like when a man sees a beautiful woman and she captures his attention in such a way that he doesn't see anybody or anything else. Many of us seem to have that same attraction, only it's to our own lives and ourselves.

We need to look outside of ourselves. We need to pay attention to the image bearers all around us. What are some ways you can love the people you run into every day? Can you make their day, buy them a meal, tell them about Christ?

What are the greatest needs in your community? Are there local missions or ministries you can serve alongside? Is your church engaged in any mercy ministry in your city?

Pray

Pray that God would give you the kind of compassion that glorifies Him and points to the good news of Jesus. Pray that God would meet the needs you become aware of in your neighborhood or at your job. The greatest way to serve people is to pray that God will meet their needs.

Serve

Be willing to sacrifice your time, money, and gifts for the good of others. We should actively be looking for ways to serve, aware that doing so will take our time. The compassion of Jesus wasn't limited to observation, but it showed itself in sacrificial action. Are you willing to give anything up so that others can gain something? We all should be.

The symptom of an encounter with the compassion of Jesus is compassion for others. If that compassion doesn't exist, you should take a hard look at your heart. Because if Jesus has shown you compassion, it's impossible not to spread it to others. Have you been exposed?

17

TURN ON THE LIGHTS

I wonder if you've ever thought about the big role light plays in our lives. As I type this, my MacBook screen is backlit, and the keys under my fingers are lit up as well. The light fixture on the ceiling of my study is shining brightly so I can see the Bible in my lap. The porch light is on right outside my house so that my wife won't trip up the steps when she returns home from a girls' night out. On her drive home the car's headlights, as well as the streetlights, will illuminate the road. As you read these words, there's either light shining down on the page or illuminating your screen. What is our obsession with light?

I don't have any deep philosophical answers for that question. It's pretty simple: when there's no light, we can't see. This is why little kids are afraid of the dark, imagining that monsters are crouching in the shadows. This is why most crime happens at night, when criminals can hide because their deeds can't be seen. This is why we stub our toes when we get up for a drink of water in the middle of the night. We depend on light for almost every moment of our lives.

But there are some people for whom light makes absolutely no difference: blind people. It's not that all the lights shut off when they enter the room, but when you can't see, light can't help you. You could shine a light into blind eyes and there would be no squints or wrinkling of the forehead. Light helps us see, but it doesn't cure blindness.

There is a light much more important than lamps and flashlights. Scripture says, "God is light, and in him is no darkness" (1 John 1:5). Scripture teaches that Jesus is the true light who came to earth to enlighten us, and that He's the radiance of the glory of God. But sadly, unless our eyes are open, we can't see that light. And there's nothing more tragic than not being able to see the very thing that the world was created to show off. And that's the glory of God.

Drug addicts get high because they don't grasp the glory of God. Rappers blaspheme His name and put themselves on a level with Jesus because they don't grasp the glory of God.

Young guys in our communities shoot each other because they don't grasp the glory of God. Young ladies put their trust in relationships because they don't grasp the glory of God. Depressed youth commit suicide because they have no hope because they don't grasp the glory of God. People go to hell because they haven't seen the glory of God in the gospel and trusted in Christ. Seeing the glory of God matters, and we want them to see it.

Where the glorious light of Christ is not seen, sins are not forgiven and souls are not saved. *This* is why we share the good news. The end goal of evangelism is that people would see the glory of God and worship Him forever. So we tell others the gospel. We can't open their eyes and shine the light of God's glory in their direction, but we can point them in His direction and ask God to give them sight.

NECESSARY BUT HARD

Telling people about Jesus is something we know we should do, yet we feel like we don't do it enough. This past week I felt convicted because a relationship I began to build with one of my neighbors has fallen off. I haven't been very intentional about building that relationship and continuing to try to tell him about Jesus. I don't think I'm alone here. It seems like we feel this way often. The question I want to ask is: Why?

Why should we preach the gospel? We open our mouths and nobody wants to hear it. People hate us for it. People say we're behind the times. People say we're clinging to an old, outdated book with outdated ideas. We live in a dark, hostile world. So why? Are we wasting our time?

We have to know why we're doing it or we'll give up. Are we preaching the gospel so we can force everybody to be like us? Is it because we're bigots who think we're better than everybody else? Is it because we all need some kind of hope to cling to and Jesus will do? No. We preach the gospel because we want people to see the glory of God. And that glory is seen in His Son.

REJECTION

Rejection is difficult. We've all experienced it. It's natural for people to be discouraged and hurt when they offer something to somebody and they get turned down. From seventh-grade boys asking a girl to a dance, to being rejected by a college, to being passed over for that new job—rejection is hard.

The apostle Paul dealt with plenty of rejection and opposition in his ministry of the gospel. So much so that in many of his letters he was forced to defend his character, his methods, and his message. But how did he respond? He said, "Therefore, having this ministry by the mercy of God, we do not lose heart" (2 Cor. 4:1).

He said he wasn't discouraged despite the fact that he faced such opposition. He didn't get depressed, give up and throw in the towel, or find something else to give his life to. He didn't retire and decide to make tents full time—which is amazing, considering everything Paul went through: imprisonments, slander, stoning, and much more. He still didn't lose heart, which is exactly what we would be tempted to do.

Have you ever shared the gospel with someone and they rejected it? I have. I can think of times when people said they didn't need God, or they argued with me and told me God wasn't real. I can think of times when people started to act weird and avoid me after I shared with them, and some people even aggressively yelled and threatened me. How would you be tempted to respond to that? Maybe you'd be tempted to fight, but I can't fight, so that's not an option for me. Most of us are tempted to fall into discouragement or cowardice and give up. Who wants to keep running into a brick wall?

When I read Paul's words saying he didn't lose heart, I want to know why. He told us right here: "Therefore, having this ministry by the mercy of God, we do not lose heart" (2 Cor. 4:1). Paul didn't lose heart because of the greatness of the ministry that God had given him.

Paul's encouragement came from the ministry itself, not from how successful he felt at any given time. He was blown away that God chose him to serve in that way. He felt privileged. As the people of God, our joy is not based on how people respond to the message. It's based on the glory of the calling itself.

So we should not lose heart. I don't mean that we shouldn't be grieved at the darkness of our world. I only mean that we shouldn't be dejected and throw in the towel. They may reject the message, but that doesn't make it any less glorious. Don't waiver. Don't lose heart.

RENOUNCE DISGRACEFUL WAYS

Paul then said, "But we have renounced disgraceful, under-handed ways. We refuse to practice cunning or to tamper with God's word" (2 Cor. 4:2). Or as the NIV puts it, "We do not use deception, nor do we distort the word of God."

Paul may have been accused of being dirty and self-seeking, so he defended himself, saying, "Nope, we've renounced that. We're not hiding things and being slimy in the way we operate."

Paul also emphasized that he refused to tamper with God's Word. When we think of people tampering with God's Word, we often think of false preachers, but you don't have to be a pastor or a TV preacher to distort the Word. What are some of the ways you may be tempted to tamper with the gospel? Making it seem more palatable? Not talking about sin? Promising people things Jesus didn't promise them? Whatever that temptation may be, you should work hard to fight it.

Tampering with the gospel reveals how you actually feel about it. Have you ever been at a banquet or a dinner and taken a sip of the iced tea, only to discover it's unsweetened? Don't you hate that? Why does unsweetened iced tea even exist? Nobody likes it. So what do you do about this atrocity? You take like eighteen sugar packets and try to make it sweet, because unsweetened tea is worthless.

In a similar manner, people see the gospel as unpalat-able, not sweet enough to people's taste buds. So they add to it. They figure as long as they don't totally get rid of it, it's fine. They just want to mix something else in there with it, to make people like it more. A dash of self-help and a teaspoon of promised prosperity. This is a horrible thing to do! And it reveals how you truly see the gospel.

You don't feel the need to tamper with something unless you think it's flawed or insufficient. Any attempt to mess with the Word is an assault on God and the way that He saves. Instead, Paul said he would "state the truth plainly" (2 Cor. 4:2, author's paraphrase).

It doesn't do anybody any good to trick them into professing faith. Adding to the truth produces veils; it doesn't remove them. If you want to appreciate a woman's beauty, the last thing you would do is cover her face with a veil. It doesn't make her more attractive; it hides her true beauty. Don't try to put makeup on the gospel to make it cute. Simply let it loose so that the true glory of Christ can shine through.

People need to see Jesus for who He actually is. But why do people seem so blind when we share this message? It feels like someone is working against us.

BEWARE THE WORK OF SATAN

There are many misconceptions about Satan. Some people go to one extreme, thinking that Satan is basically all-powerful. Everything that happens is a result of his great power, and he can do whatever he wants whenever he wants to do it. Then there are some who go to the other extreme, imagining that

Satan doesn't exist, or that he's powerless and inactive. Both of these extremes are lies, and they are dangerous for us to believe.

The truth is, Satan does have power. He had enough power to work against Paul and his ministry: "And even if our gospel is veiled, it is veiled to those who are perishing. In their case the god of this world has blinded the minds of the unbelievers, to keep them from seeing the light of the gospel of the glory of Christ, who is the image of God" (2 Cor. 4:3–4).

Paul called Satan the "god of this world," so it's clear that he has some power, but not all power. He's called the god of this world or this age, and only this age. Paul said the people who were perishing couldn't see because Satan blinded them.

This should be evidence of how amazing and important it is for us to see the glory of God. One of Satan's main goals is to keep us from seeing it. Satan goes so far as to blind us to make sure we cannot see the glory of God in the gospel.

Some of us wonder why our world is so dark right now. Why people are so sinful, hateful toward one another, and hostile toward God. Well, here's the answer: they're blind. Maybe you've been sharing with a friend or a family member for years with no progress and you're tired. It seems impossible. We shouldn't get frustrated and give up on people. If God can save you, He can save anyone! If God can save me, He can save anyone. They are blind, and they need to see. So let's help them see.

This also shows us that when people reject the gospel, it's

not because the message is flawed. Don't let rejection make you doubt the Word. The fact that blind people can't see how beautiful the *Mona Lisa* is doesn't mean it's not beautiful. We don't base our opinions of art on people who can't see. And the beauty of the gospel is not determined by those who can't behold it.

PREACH JESUS

One of the reasons many of us struggle with evangelism is that we misunderstand what we've been called to do. Paul said, "For what we proclaim is not ourselves, but Jesus Christ as Lord, with ourselves as your servants for Jesus' sake" (2 Cor. 4:5).

When people don't believe, they aren't rejecting me, but Him. As a minister of the gospel, you have one primary task: proclaim Christ. We get bogged down, confused, and discouraged because we get away from the main thing. Tell people about Jesus.

When you come into contact with somebody who's lost, without hope, and without God, and you ask yourself what you should do, tell that person about Jesus. That's what they need. Yes, they have other needs. But their main need is Jesus.

If you truly want men to see the glory of God, it does them no good to preach other things. Now, that doesn't mean you shouldn't help people live their lives well; it just means Christ has to be at the center of that. If Jesus is not the foundation, the motivation, the fuel behind everything else we preach, what we're doing won't last.

What does it mean to preach Christ? We know from the rest of the text and elsewhere in the Scriptures that Paul was referring to the gospel message. Paul said to the Corinthians, "I decided to know nothing among you except Jesus Christ and him crucified" (1 Cor. 2:2). Paul meant the message about Jesus, what He's done, and how He saves.

At the core of this gospel message is the truth that God is holy, man is sinful, Christ was perfect and died for sinners, and He rose from the grave. And those who turn from sin and trust in Christ will be saved. That's the message you've been called to preach.

POWER

Recently I heard two testimonies from believers in my church. These two people had very different stories. One was a drug dealer who had been locked up. Another was a good girl who hated God. Both of them had heard the gospel many times, but they felt no affection for Christ and they did not believe it. Time and time again they rejected God's offer of mercy. Do you want to know what finally moved them to trust Christ? Someone else shared the gospel with them *again*. We never know when God is going to work or how God is going to work. We just need to do our job. Tell people about Jesus so they can see the glory of Jesus.

Some of us like to share our testimonies, which is good.

But when the gospel isn't present, we're proclaiming self, not Christ. "I was a crackhead, then I wasn't." That's a nice story, but how can I be saved? Whether you mean to or not, that's preaching yourself. We are doing the very thing Paul said he did *not* do. Please do share your testimony, but tell about the good news that saved you.

SERVING THOSE WHO NEED THE TRUTH

In what ways have you been sharing the gospel lately? Who have you been sharing with? What do you talk about when you sit in the barber chair or at the beauty salon? What do you say to your neighbors or your coworkers or your fellow students when you get a few minutes to talk about things?

Are you, like Paul, making yourself the servant of those who need to hear the good news? For somebody to hear the gospel from me, does it have to be the perfect situation? Do they have to bring a Bible to my bedroom and open to John 3:16? I hope not. I want to be intentional and even inconvenience myself so that others will get to meet Christ.

Some of us are too busy. We work a lot, or we serve at church a lot, and we don't ever spend time with non-Christians. Sometimes I feel like I haven't had any opportunities to share about Christ in a while. But we shouldn't leave telling people about Christ up to chance. We should build our lives around evangelism. We should make sacrifices to tell people about Christ.

Who will go to another country to share the good news?

There are people who don't know. There are people who are blind. Where are the urban missionaries willing to go across the world? And if people are blind, what's the point of going?

HOPE IN THE WORK OF GOD

If the world being saved depends on us, it is literally impossible. We can't open blind eyes. All we can do is preach and love on them. Is God asking us to do the impossible? Maybe.

Jesus said to Paul, "I am sending you to them to open their eyes and turn them from darkness to light, and from the power of Satan to God, so that they may receive forgiveness of sins and a place among those who are sanctified by faith in me" (Acts 26:17–18 NIV). How is that possible? Man can't do that. Look at 2 Corinthians 4:6: "For God, who said, 'Let light shine out of darkness,' has shone in our hearts to give the light of the knowledge of the glory of God in the face of Jesus Christ."

Paul took a moment to remind us who God is. He wanted to give us a quick reminder of His track record. This is not a God who's trying to do something amazing for the first time. This is not a God who was born yesterday or even a million years ago. This is not a God who was created. This is not a God whose hands are tied by the so-called god of this world. The God we're going to other people on behalf of is the same God who created absolutely everything from absolutely nothing.

If He can create all creation with mere words, He can bring blind dead men to life. Blind eyes are no match for our God. Wicked minds are no match for our God. Dark hearts are no match for our God. He said, "Let there be light" once and He can say it again. That's the point Paul was making.

Christian, if you've seen the glory of God in the face of Jesus, if you've turned from darkness to light, it is not your doing. It's not ultimately the doing of the person who shared with you. It's God's doing. Only God can do that. While the god of this world blinds us from the glory of Jesus, the true and living God shines light into hearts and opens blind eyes. And He uses His Word to do it.

Do you grasp what God has done for you? A lot of us, including myself, are not passionate enough about evangelism because we're not grateful enough that we get to gaze at the glory of God in the gospel. If we were more captured and enthralled with our God and what we have in Christ, we would tell other people more. We tell them about shows we like and good albums and conferences. Do we tell them about Jesus? When we love something, we can't help but share it with others.

KEEP PREACHING

Ministry in this fallen, dark world has never been and never will be easy. But we can learn from Paul's example in 2 Corinthians 4. Passages like that keep the weighty reality of evangelism at the forefront of our minds.

There are really only two options for us when this life is over. Those of us who have not put our faith in Christ will perish. But if we turn and trust in Christ, we get to see a glimpse of His glory now in the gospel. And later, after He returns, all of us will get new bodies. And we will gaze at His glory in its fullness forever. Brothers and sisters, there is a lot at stake. Keep preaching the gospel so people can see His glory.

18

BE A REAL MEMBER

I went to a Bible college. Bible college is a great place to be when you're doing well spiritually, but it's possibly the worst place to be if you're doing terrible spiritually. Why do I say that? Because whether or not you have any desire to read your Bible, or go to chapel, or think about God, you're still forced to go through all the motions. It's a very strange place to be for many people, which is why Bible college or seminary can be destructive seasons for so many people. The problem isn't biblical education, though—it's studying God's Word theoretically instead of devotionally.

One of the strangest things about Bible college for me was the way many students treated the church. There was a class on the nature and purpose of the local church that every student was required to take, partly because many of the students wanted to be pastors or missionaries. Most of the students were bright and understood their Bibles pretty well. But so many also treated church like an add-on instead of a practice at the core of what it means to follow Jesus. Church membership was treated like an option instead of a necessity.

The school had a rule about attending a church each Sunday, and students were required to log their church attendance. The school made sure students were going every Sunday by taking attendance as if it were a class. I appreciate what the school was trying to do, but I wonder how effective it was, considering I knew a lot of students who fabricated their attendance sheets. They pretended to go to church so that they wouldn't have to face the consequences. I was baffled.

This disinterest in the church was puzzling to me because God had recently begun curing me of some of that disinterest. There was never a point as a Christian where I thought church was stupid or a waste of time, but there was a time when I saw it as just another good thing a Christian should do. The church's role in my life was minimal and peripheral instead of paramount and central. The Lord used faithful Bible teaching to correct my perspective.

Seeing in others a lack of affection for the church grieved me because God was in the process of giving me a deep affection for His people. I was growing like crazy, and I wanted to help other people grow too. The church was more than a cool place to go; it was the people I did life with. I was sad that people were missing out on something so great!

Only a minority of students lied about their church attendance, but many others weren't committed to any church. Many attended regularly, but they never got involved in the life of those churches. They simply showed up on Sundays, sang songs, listened to sermons, shook some hands, and headed home. They never became members, they never made a commitment to love anyone, and no one made a commitment to keep watch over their souls.

This isn't just an issue with Bible college students, though; it seems to be a college problem in general. Why won't we commit ourselves to loving God's church?

At this point of the chapter I want to specifically address those who are college age and above. If you happen to be reading this book and you're younger (i.e., a teenager living at home with your parents), this will likely be a different conversation for you. I think you can, however, still benefit from thinking about these things.

DO WE SELL OURSELVES SHORT?

Let's be real with ourselves. Twentysomethings are definitely not known for filling up churches on Sunday mornings. Church growth gurus see us as the hard-to-reach age. We're old enough to make our own decisions but often too young to make mature ones. Some of us still haven't realized the emptiness of the world and the fullness available in the church, so we keep a safe distance between the church and us. We don't run away altogether, but we don't fully embrace it either, kind of like kids at a junior high dance.

Whatever the reason for our absence, many churches are discouraged that their attempts to reach us keep failing. Many of them pray for us and strategize to meet our needs. Other churches have given up hope altogether, so their attempts to reach us are nonexistent. What's the problem here? Are they just out of touch with our generation?

I do think part of the problem is that churches often want to segregate young people into the spiritual ghetto: for example, college and singles ministry. Those kinds of ministries are definitely fruitful in many churches, but they're not enough. It's a shame to see, but sometimes the churches aren't treating us like real Christians who are part of the life of the whole church. Instead, we're like minor league pitchers, waiting for our chance to be called up to the big leagues one day. Who wants that?

While ministry segregation is definitely a problem, it's not the only issue at work. Many of us need to look in the mirror and point the finger at our own reflections.

JOIN THE BUILDING PROJECT

Our lack of commitment to God's people is one way we feed the lie that young people are not real people or real Christians yet. We say we're followers of Jesus, yet many of us have no interest in doing some of the most basic acts of following Him, like joining a church. We prefer to bounce around or tell ourselves that we're waiting until we're more settled. But is that acceptable?

When Paul wrote to Timothy, he made sure to remind him that his youthfulness was in no way an obstacle to his faithfulness. Paul told him that he didn't have to graduate to the next stage before he could be a faithful leader in God's church; instead, he should glorify God right where he was. Paul encouraged Timothy to be an example for the believers, specifically the believers in that community. You, too, as a member of a church, are to be an example for the other believers in that church. Not just believers your age, either, but believers in all stages of life.

Many of us spend our young-adult years as regular attenders of campus ministries and other age-specific events, where we hear the Word preached and fellowship with Christian friends. We should praise God for providing those things, but none of them are enough. Podcasting your favorite preacher is not enough. Anything less than what God intends is not enough. God has given us the church, and we should drink deeply from that fountain of grace. And not only has He given the church to us, but He's also given us to the church.

God gave us gifts to build up His church, but we're not close enough or involved enough to do so. We're like a construction worker parking outside the site and watching what the rest of the workers are doing. He may be physically present, but his presence is in no way helping them construct that building.

The church is God's construction project, being built up into mature personhood in Christ. And He builds that body through its various members. You are a brick and so am I. We cannot serve God's church the way we are meant to from the outside. We must be in the life of the body so that we can serve them as we are meant to.

CHURCH MEMBERSHIP IN THE BIBLE

Before we go any further, I want to address the question that many may be asking: Why does this guy keep talking about membership? Is that even in the Bible? That's a good question, and the short answer is yes.

There is no place in Ephesians where Paul said, "Tell everyone to pursue formal membership or else." But it is assumed and implied. Paul wrote letters to churches about how they should interact with one another, not to random people about how they should interact with other random people. Saying membership isn't in Paul's letters is like me writing a letter to the Johnson family and someone saying there are no commands for family in there. Well, you're already a family, and I wrote to you about how to interact with one another. Isn't family kind of assumed?

Beyond that, it may be helpful if we define *membership*, since it brings different things to mind for each of us.

Membership is the word we use to summarize our relationships within a local church. I don't mean mere friendships. How does God say we are to relate to one another, and what does that commitment look like? What's the relationship between you, other members, and the leadership of the church? The sum of those relationships and commitments is what I'm calling "membership."

God has called you to love other Christians, serve them, and commit yourself to them. He has called you to support and submit to the pastors in a local church. God has called those other Christians likewise to commit themselves to loving you and submitting to those leaders. And God has called those pastors to love all of you, preach the Word, shepherd the flock, and be accountable to you. Membership is the name we use to summarize those relationships and commitments.

It's like a family. We may show love to neighbors and friends, but there is something special about our parents and siblings. Being a *member* of the family is what you call that unique relationship. You live together, love each other, and share flesh and blood.

Of course, we're not all related, but we willingly commit ourselves to one another. Scripture commands us to encourage one another, spur one another on, restore one another, and sing songs to one another. The truth is, you cannot obey these "one another" commands without real commitment to a church. And churches will suffer from the lack of young people. Who's going to share the gospel with the young people you run into every day? And who's going to connect them to other believers? Our churches need us.

LOVING VS. LEECHING

Many young people do attend church regularly, but they don't do anything. They come, hear the message, sing the songs, and go home. They aren't serving anyone, and they don't know anyone. They are essentially leeches, eating but not contributing. This is not what it looks like to be a part of a body of believers.

Wouldn't it be strange if I gave you a gift but you left it wrapped? When we refuse to get involved in the life of a church, we're essentially a bunch of wrapped gifts sitting around. There are a million excuses we can come up with, but we should do whatever it takes to obey God by getting involved.

What if there's nowhere for me to serve? Don't wait for someone to give you a title or an official role to serve in the church. Just do the things that Jesus has called you to do as a Christian. Love people. Help others follow Christ. Help deacons meet physical needs in your church. Just be obedient!

If joining a church seems more like a nuisance than a privilege, that could be evidence you still have some growing to do. It's much more than an annoying necessity in God's eyes. And I want to encourage you to be excited about the things God is excited about. He loves the church, and we should love the church as well. So let's rise above the non-committal leechiness and get involved!

CONCLUSION

Spoiler Alert

It's possible to watch a phenomenal movie but still leave dissatisfied. And it's usually someone else's fault. My rowdy friends who quote their favorite lines and shout at the screen don't get invitations to watch anything with me. And it's my personal opinion that freakishly tall people should just watch movies at home—or at least slouch down so average-height moviegoers like me can enjoy the film. Loud and tall people at the movies can be annoying, but nothing ruins a movie like knowing the ending.

When you already know that the main character dies at the end, the two-hour emotional roller coaster seems pointless. And if you know they survive, your heart won't really pound when they're being chased. Knowing the ending takes all the suspense out of the experience. Spoilers almost always ruin a good story, but I can think of at least one story where knowing the ending makes it better—my own story and yours.

OUR STORY IN HIS STORY

Our daily lives seem to be marked by lots of suspense and plenty of ups and downs. Some of our stories make movie dramas look like a Charlie Brown comic. Our stories are filled with disappointment and undesired outcomes, and we can be tempted to wonder if our stories end with disaster. But believers don't have to wonder. God has told us in His Word exactly where our stories end:

> Beloved, we are God's children now, and what we will be has not yet appeared; but we know that when he appears we shall be like him, because we shall see him as he is. (1 John 3:2)

> Just as we have borne the image of the man of dust, we shall also bear the image of the man of heaven. (1 Cor. 15:49)

Blessed be the God and Father of our Lord Jesus Christ! According to his great mercy, he has caused us to be born again to a living hope through the resurrection of Jesus Christ from the dead, to an inheritance that is imperishable, undefiled, and unfading, kept in heaven for you, who by God's power are being guarded through faith for a salvation ready to be revealed in the last time. (1 Peter 1:3–5)

Passages like these are a tremendous encouragement to me. When I look at my life now, I'm painfully aware of my own sin. There are areas in my life where God has grown me, but those aren't the areas I think about at the end of the day. I'm usually fighting to remember that I'm forgiven by Jesus, because all I can think about are the areas where I still fall short.

As this book concludes, I don't want you to be discouraged. Reading so much about what God has called us to can be a painful reminder of how far we have to go. I once heard a preacher say that for every time you look at yourself, you should take two looks at the cross. I think that's good advice.

When I look at my life now, I see focus, but I also see confusion. I see healing, but I also see brokenness. I see growth, but I also see sin. All our life stories are full of ups and downs. We have times of great joy and great sorrow. Most of us will go through seasons during which all we see is pain, and everywhere we look there's nothing to hold on to. We would be left hopeless, wondering where we'll end up—except God has already told us how our stories end. God wins. And because we've been drafted onto His squad, we win.

In the tumultuous story that is my real life, I don't want suspense—I want assurance. I don't want any cliffhangers; I want to know what happens. That gives me strength to fight. We know the Lord has already gone before us in battle, but that doesn't mean we don't fight. It just means we can't lose.

NOTES

Chapter 1: 7:00 a.m. Logic
1. Taylor Swift, "22," *Red*, Big Machine Records, 2012.

Chapter 4: There Are No Super-Christians
1. Lady Gaga, "Born This Way," *Born This Way*, Interscope Records, 2011.
2. Jay-Z and Kanye West, "Made in America," *Watch the Throne*, Def Jam, 2011.
3. Macklemore and Ryan Lewis, "Same Love," *The Heist*, Macklemore, 2012.

Chapter 7: Not Guilty by Association

1. Kendrick Lamar, "The Art of Peer Pressure," *good kid, m.A.A.d city*, Aftermath, 2012.

Chapter 11: Age Is More than Just a Number

1. John Mayer, "Stop This Train," *Continuum*, Aware/Columbia, 2006.

Chapter 12: The Grey Rule

1. Ted Turnau, *Popologetics: Popular Culture in Christian Perspective* (Phillipsburg, NJ: P & R Publishing, 2012), 215.

Chapter 13: Rude Awakening

1. Christopher Hitchens, *Mortality* (Toronto: McClelland and Stewart, 2012), 59–60.

Chapter 14: Are You One of Those Christians?

1. David Sedaris, *Let's Explore Diabetes with Owls* (New York: Back Bay Books, 2014), 73–74.

Chapter 15: Everything Is Sacred

1. "Alan Moore Interview Part 1 2013," YouTube video, 5:21, posted by "NorthamptonCollege01," February 26, 2013, http://www.youtube.com/watch?v=kCPZdLgOXUY.

ABOUT THE AUTHOR

Trip Lee is an author, hip-hop artist, pastor, and thought leader. He regularly preaches and teaches at Christian conferences and events and has performed his music for thousands of listeners around the world. As a critically acclaimed hip-hop artist, Trip has won a Stellar Award and been nominated for several Dove awards. His latest album is entitled *Rise*. He and Jessica, his wife of five years, have two young children.

builttobrag.com
@TripLee

RISE

NEW ALBUM
FROM TRIP LEE
IN STORES NOW